My Journey to

Soaring to N

Scott E. Harlow

ISBN: 979-8-89212-423-2

Dedication

First and foremost, I dedicate this book to my beautiful girls, Madison and Jacie, who have stood by me through thick and thin. Their unwavering support and refusal to give up on me have been a beacon of strength. My love for them is unconditional, and I am profoundly grateful for their enduring presence in my life.

I extend this dedication to the rest of my family and friends, who have been a guiding light during my darkest days. A special acknowledgment goes to John and Amanda, who generously opened their home to me for nearly two years, providing unwavering support without judgment. I am beyond grateful for their sincerity and kindness, which have made a significant impact on my journey.

Lastly, this book is dedicated to all those who have been a major support to my entire family during both good and challenging times. Your steadfast support merits the best that life has to offer, and I extend my heartfelt appreciation for your enduring presence.

Me with my amazing girls

Acknowledgment

I express my sincere appreciation to the book publication team for their steadfast support throughout the entire process. I am grateful for the team's professional expertise in organization and their thorough assistance in bringing this book to publication.

Overall, the experience has been truly memorable, given the accurate and professional handling of every aspect. The team's positive attitude has not only provided me with hope but also a sense of assurance throughout the journey.

I am thankful for the collective efforts of each team member, and the seamless collaboration has made this endeavor both rewarding and successful. The commitment to excellence and attention to detail have shaped the outcome of this book, making it a testament to the dedication of the entire team.

About the Author

Scott Eric Harlow is a dedicated full-time businessman specializing in window film and real estate investments. In addition to his business pursuits, Harlow holds certifications with QuickBooks accounting and addiction counseling. He is also an FAA-licensed pilot.

Born and raised in a Christian family, his passion for adventure and travel traces back to his childhood. During his early years, he engaged in a variety of outdoor activities, including boating, cycling, skiing, swimming, and hiking—however, his desire for flying developed at the age of 14 through flying gliders. He eventually developed his love for the sky as a professional skydiver and private pilot.

Contents

Chapter 1: The Beginning

My parents were high school sweethearts. They met in a dance class and were inseparable. They were the type of young love people talk about in books and see in movies. The type where they would feel a sea of emotions for each other every time they looked into each other's eyes. They both grew up in New England, while my maternal grandmother was from Newfoundland, Canada. My father and mother both loved the outdoors and were adventurers. My dad loved and taught ballroom dancing and was extremely passionate about it. He even taught my siblings how to ballroom dance when they were younger. To my parent's disappointment, I had no interest in it.

My father (Richard Lee Harlow) worked at a bank in Boston when he met the love of his life. He started working at the bank as a messenger boy but rose through the ranks and became the bank's Vice President. He was a dedicated man who put all of his hard work into that company and worked there for 37 years before taking early retirement at 55. He loved spending time with cousins in Putney, Vermont at the family apple, berry and maple syrup farm..." Harlow's Sugar House". He took me with him many times. On the other hand, my mother wanted to be a writer ever since she could write. Even when she was a kid, if anyone asked her what she wanted to be, she would always say that she wanted to become a writer and that conviction and determination led her to become a successful and published author today. She is currently 91 and lives in Florida.

My mother (Joan Beverly Hiatt Harlow) became a remarkable children's author and has written many [1]books, which have also been published by significant publishers like Margaret K. McElderry Books. Her acclaimed books, magazine stories, and articles have appeared in major children's publications. Several of those books are based on my grandmother and her experiences in Newfoundland. The books are mostly fictional, with elements of my mother's personal life sprinkled in there to make them inimitable.

When I was around 9, we drove to Newfoundland, where my grandmother (Marguerite Small Hiatt) was born, in Moreton's Harbor. I thought of it as a great vacation, not knowing that it inspired my mother to base several characters in her books around her trip experiences. All the characters in her stories were based on some of the amazing people she met on her trip.

[1] http://www.joanhiattharlow.com/

Although she was a children's fiction writer, she firmly believed that you could find such unique characteristics in everyday life, too.

As kids, she encouraged all of us to write poetry. With her help, we all wrote poems that were published in a book titled "Poems Are for Everything."

My parents lived a great life, although my dad passed away over 20 years ago, at age 70, from complications with Parkinson's disease. They had five kids and tried their best to create a memorable life for all of us. We had a yearly tradition where my mom would get permission from our school so that we could take the entire month of April off. We would take our homework with us, excited to spend our days at the beach. I would usually finish all my work within the first few days so that I could stop worrying about it. We would stay at Florida beaches and play every day.

I would walk miles up and down the beach to look for fossils and find interesting things, including shark teeth, sea fossils, and things that shouldn't be in the sea, like a camel's tooth or a horse's tooth. I once even found pieces of a mammoth tooth. We identified all of these at a local library, which was surprising and a great story to tell all my friends back in school.

Me in third grade.

When I was in 3rd grade, my family got into skiing. We would go on the weekends or take time off school to go. I would sometimes go with my father, or we would go as a family a couple of times; it wasn't as much fun for me when we went as a family as when I would go with only one parent.

Me and my family members

My young brain couldn't decipher why, but I noticed that my parents would start arguing sometimes when they were together, dampening everyone's mood. Sometimes, they were just mean to each other and would belittle each other. That's when I noticed it was more fun not having my father around, but I quickly realized that I shouldn't say that as a kid.

Going on trips with my mom was always an adventure. My mother was always seeking adventures. We once went to visit my sister and see her kids in California, and my mother was so excited that she selected our route so we could go to space observatories along the way. We visited two observatories, and let me tell you, looking at the night sky through a giant telescope was a breathtaking and surreal experience that I will never forget. We got to see the night sky's magnificence truly—one in Arizona and the other in California. The experience was so great that my dad gave my mom a telescope as an anniversary gift, which she shared with all of us.

I remember being very irritable during the whole drive there, which I now believe was the typical behavior of a teenager. My teenage brain couldn't fathom the need for my father to stop every hour to take a break and walk for 15 minutes. My sister, Jen, breathing over my shoulder from the back seat, often drove me crazy. It felt like we were never going to get there. We also visited the Grand Canyon during that trip, which was amazing. I wished we could have stayed there longer to explore. My mother and younger sister ended up getting sick with coughs, so we needed to move on.

When we arrived in California, my sister Lisa broke the news that my grandfather (Albert Hiatt) had just passed away. Between the sad news and the bad coughs, our trip was dampened. On the bright side, we were happy to meet our new extended family, which made me an uncle to 2 more nephews, Rusty and Brandon. (My first nephew was Justin, my oldest sister Debbie's firstborn.) My dad flew home to take care of the funeral arrangements.

On the way back, my mother had a kink in her neck, where she couldn't fully turn her head, but she persevered and drove the entire way back. We stopped for a couple of nights as she was in extreme pain throughout the journey. I acted as her speed detector, but after a while, I wouldn't remind her until her speed crossed 85. She even let me drive for a while to give her some rest from all the driving, even though I was around 14-15 at the time. I loved to drive, and I didn't get caught, which was a great thrill and was all that mattered at the time.

My parents have taught me a lot about how to live life. Although they had their own vices like the rest of us, they always tried their best to give us a memorable childhood by taking us for outdoor activities like swimming, boating, hiking, and skiing. They showed their affection by taking us on adventures and making memories with us, which stayed with me.

I now look back on those memories fondly, especially after losing my father in 2002.

Chapter 2: Early Life

My Sisters

Having four sisters, three older, Debbie, Kristan, and Lisa, and one younger than me, Jennifer, is a blessing for which I will always be grateful.

I was ecstatic when my youngest sister, Jennifer, came into our lives. Because of her birth, I was not only able to rid myself of the title of the baby of the family, but I was also a very proud older brother who wanted to protect his sister from any dangers of life.

My siblings and I are four to five years apart. My oldest sister, Debbie, is 12 years older than me. She got married to Paul when I was only 7. She moved in with Paul to their first apartment together after the wedding and had their first son, Justin, when I was 12

She has always been a loving and supportive influence to all of us. My relationship with her blossomed over the years as her family grew to a family of four. Two handsome sons, Justin and Adam. She also has two grandsons, Jackson and Samuel.

Just two years ago, Debbie was diagnosed with lung cancer. She was never a smoker, but fortunately, it was discovered soon enough that she had been stable after surgery and chemo. Her faith in God, combined with a positive attitude and resilience, keeps carrying her along.

Interestingly, my first job was with Paul when I was in high school. Kristan was a true example of a middle child. Although she is between Lisa and me, she acted like one would believe a middle child would behave. Even as a young kid, Kristan always did what she wanted and didn't wait for the family's approval.

Once she put her mind to anything, she didn't let anyone's opinion dictate her life. At 18, Kristan joined the Army and served four years in Germany, where she met her husband. She has a beautiful daughter named Stephanie and a grandson named Richie, named after my dad. I became close with her and her husband when she came back from Germany. Her marriage was seemingly doing perfectly fine. However, it shocked me when they filed for a divorce. You don't truly know what is happening in someone's life and only know what they choose to show you.

My sisters and I remained supportive of Kristan during the painful divorce affair. After her divorce, she continued with her accounting career. While working for the government, she also owns a ballroom dance studio in Florida. Perhaps she has taken after my dad for her love for dance. Kristan met her current husband, Barry, in Florida. They run their dancing studio together and teach ballroom dance passionately. I am close to all my sisters. My third elder sister, Lisa, is seven years older than me. All of us have a special bond with her. She has an incredible sense of humor and is always thoughtful and kind to everyone, including strangers. Due to her sweet nature, Lisa loves to look after everyone around her and is the first to offer help indiscriminately to anyone in a difficult situation. Lisa loves and takes great care of the kids. Even as a kid, Lisa was always friendly and helped other kids in the neighborhood. She has two sons, Rusty and Brandon, and three grandchildren, Anthony, Hope, and Abby, whom she adores.

Despite doing good to others, Lisa had a stroke of bad luck with men, making her life challenging. Life has been unfair to her because she deserved way better than what she got. However, my sisters and I have always stood by Lisa. I am proud that my sisters are remarkably strong and caring at the same time.

My youngest sister, Jennifer, is four years younger than me. She came around when we had just moved into our house in Chelmsford. Jen and I played well together. I loved the weather and still do. We had fun pretending to be meteorologists and recorded our weather reports on cassette. We stuck together all through our childhood, loved playing pranks, and teased each other. All of my sisters enjoyed teasing me. During her short-lived marriage, she gave birth to Joshua. Later in life, she had a grandson, Owen. Currently, she has been happily married to Joe for about 25 years and has a beautiful daughter, Jordan.

Looking back, growing up as the only boy amongst five siblings, I didn't realize how lucky I was and the many things I took for granted.

Familial Bond

Growing up, I only had a few friends around the neighborhood. I played by myself most of the time and seldom played with the kids in the neighborhood when I was young. It may be because I already had four sisters, so I didn't need many friends. When my grandmother bought a bike for me, I walked it through the neighborhood alone at first. But before long, I learned how to ride it as other kids joined me.

I loved the violin and viola and played it from elementary school through high school. In grade 3, I was enrolled in music classes at school, where I made friends. I found people with similar interests and instantly bonded with them. I could communicate with them easily as we could bond on something we had in common. And even after decades, that bond remains intact with some of those friends.

I loved the snow and shoveling. I loved it so much that I shoveled neighbors' driveways for pay. I got upset when people would walk through the yard and make footprints, "wrecking" the smooth blanket of snow. I loved it even more for skiing. There is nothing like skiing on fresh powder snow.

***

Once, I heard a noise and then a scream. I ran into the room to find Jennifer stuck to a fan. Her hair had somehow gotten into the fan and was completely twisted to the point that the fan could barely move, and her head was stuck to the fan. It was funny! I laughed so hard at how the fan was still trying to turn, and her face was so taut that it looked like she got a facelift. I eventually helped her get out of the fan just after I finished laughing. We always reminisce about this and other similar memories, which makes us chuckle to this day.

I spent a lot of time with my family growing up. Our yearly trips to Florida were extremely fun. We would spend all day swimming, body surfing, and looking for fossils on the beach. During the long drive there, we would break it up by exploring different places, such as Luray Caverns, Amish Country, Blue Ridge Mountains, Washington DC, Disney, and more.

Great memories of skiing with my family and teaching my youngest sister (and my own kids) how to ski are special to me. Although I was the only one in my family who got passionate about skiing after I grew up, our family skiing trips were truly unforgettable. The most memorable times we spent together as a family were at the lake house. We would walk on the dirt road and see deer, foxes, raccoons, and an occasional moose while enjoying the nature surrounding us. We spent days, weekends, and summers together there, strengthening our familial bond. I will always fondly remember our time at the camp. Being away from society and free of our daily routines helped to keep us close together. We would also spend lots of time on the boat, swimming, fishing, grocery shopping, and even dinner and ice cream.

Our lake house

Being away from society and free of our daily routines helped bring us closer than ever before. The camp was generational. My grandparents built it in the 1940s and handed it down to five generations.

Lake Winnipesaukee: My favorite place on earth

It was my favorite place on earth, with all of my memories going back to infancy, and the same goes for my own children. We also shared it with friends and extended family. It was a painful loss when it had to be sold a few years ago.

My Family Struggle and Support

Debbie's diagnosis of lung cancer was an incredibly stressful time for the entire family. Debbie underwent chemo, and half of her infected lung was removed to stop the spread of the cancer. She is stable right now and is feeling much better. We are all thankful, grateful, and hopeful for that.

All of us have struggled with depression and anxiety, which is normal. Severe cases are considered "disorders" and can be hereditary. My mother had a higher level of depression and anxiety, mostly during her younger years. I'm sure we all have had different levels of it, but I think I was hit the hardest.

My parents used to consume alcohol, which was always in our house. I believe that the exposure to alcohol at such a young age might have affected my relationship with alcohol even as an adult. I now know that alcohol did not help to solve my mental health issues, something I wouldn't have been able to admit to myself until a couple of years ago.

My siblings and I were brought up as part of the Jehovah's Witnesses, which kept us separate and provided us with a different perspective on life that taught me some eye-opening things. It wasn't forced on us; we had free will to choose our paths.

Certain significant things and experiences in my life steered me back to a stronger faith in God. I have been blessed many times, including my two beautiful daughters, and the strength and determination I didn't know I had to overcome even the biggest obstacles life has thrown at me.

Chapter 3: School Days

I switched to multiple schools, from elementary school to high school in Chelmsford, Massachusetts. The first one was The North School, where I attended elementary classes from grade 1 till grade 4.

Although I was not eager to go to school in the beginning, I was still a good student, and the teachers never had any complaints about me. I also liked most of my teachers throughout each year. I still remember their names.

Reminiscing the carefree old days always caused my eyes to sparkle. During our gym class, all the kids would hold a parachute in a circle, and the lightest people would jump in the middle and get thrown up in the air. It was exhilarating when one was thrown upward and felt like a liberated flying bird. I believe this was the first encounter with the exciting feeling that built my interest in flying.

However, one displeased school day memory that still makes me feel humiliated was when my grade 2 teacher accused me of pushing drugs. I had always wondered what caused her to say so for a grade 2 student - maybe my breath spray that stung when I squirted a little bit of it on my tongue made her think I was an addict and dealer.

One particular day, some of my schoolmates saw me spray in my mouth, and they wanted to test it out. I loved all the attention and didn't think there was any harm in doing it. So, I shared my spray with everyone else to experience the fun.

When the teacher saw us doing it, she asked how it started and went crazy. So, she accused me of pushing drugs on other kids and that I should be ashamed of myself. Then, she sent me to the nurse to tell her what I did. Even the nurse was confused about my visit and told me I hadn't done anything wrong.

When I returned from the nurse's office, she stood menacingly before me with her arms folded across her chest and frowned. Then, she started interrogating me in front of the classroom, which was humiliating and felt devastating with my entire class present as witnesses. I was crushed and didn't talk to anybody for the rest of the day. And when I got home, I hid under the table to escape the embarrassment I faced that day in school.

Seeing my unusual behavior, my parents became concerned and couldn't figure out what was wrong with me. Then, they asked me what the matter was. At first, I was scared to tell them about it, fearing that they would agree with the teacher and I would get into further trouble at home for doing drugs. However, I gathered as much courage as a seven-year-old could and told them what had transpired that day at the school. My parents were furious. They couldn't believe anyone dared to accuse a minor child of such a vile thing. They went to report the incident to the school the very next day. They threatened the teacher's job, and she knew she could be fired for falsely accusing a young child of selling drugs in front of the entire classroom.

My parent's complaint had a significant impact. Though the teacher wasn't fired, she never again did anything to me or anyone in my classroom. Imagine how badly scarred I was as a kid that I still vividly remember that traumatizing incident.

In grade 5, I was moved to a school that was a schoolhouse of its own. It was a big old house, an old school house with just four classrooms in it.

Only part of the 5th grade went there, while others went to different schools. In grade 6, we were all transferred to one school for the first time, McFarland School, the old high school building.

I had my first interaction with bullying behavior in that school. I started getting teased and annoyed by kids. It wasn't to the point that altered my life, but it was significant enough that I started noticing others' behavior towards me.

I continued to play violin and made some good friends in that school. Even though there was some minor bullying, I also met my lifelong best friend,

John, that year, who was in music class with me and played string bass. We were back to separate schools from grade 7 to grade 9. I was now in Junior high school, which meant I was surrounded by older kids, with 7th graders as the youngest in the building. I wasn't used to having older kids in the school, so I felt intimidated. And by grade 8, it kept getting more and more intimidating. Being surrounded by kids growing up and trying to find their identity, I was also struggling with my own sense of self. It can become a difficult and daunting task for a teenager. Going through puberty brings changes and an arena of varying emotions, and I struggled to regulate my emotions and feelings.

In grade 9, I went to technical high school to learn a trade. This school was in a different town and a regional school where other kids from different towns were handpicked to qualify for the school. I qualified since I had good grades and decided to switch to technical school. They had an exploratory program for the first-year students where students could try out a class to learn about plumbing and heating, carpentry, electrical, or any of the different courses taught at the school. At the end of that year, students had a choice to continue with their preference or pursue another field. I started with carpentry, and I liked it. I learned much about it and was taking in all the new information. Some vulgar guys would act as real jerks with the first-year students in that class. So, I began to dread going to school because of them. They made me want to quit school due to their constant bullying. That was the first time their bullying affected me enough that I wanted to quit something I was passionate about. I had experienced bullying before and thought I had a pretty thick skin because of it, but these kids took bullying to the next level.

Teenagers can become extremely mean assholes if they aren't guided to express empathy for everyone. Those kids were extremely harsh and would threaten me unprovoked. For some strange reason, they wanted to fight me. Several times, they approached me and said, *"Meet us in the Pines after school,"* referring to the pine forest behind our school. I was confused and asked them, *"Why?"* that made them aggressive, and they said that they would beat the shit out of me.

However, I acted very confident in front of them, as I knew they would pick on me even more if I showed fear. I told them I had better things to do than fight without reason. But deep inside, I was terrified. I didn't want to be beaten up, and I never really understood the reasoning behind their hatred.

The bullying became relentless. No matter what I tried to do to stop it, it kept getting worse. It all came to a head when we played basketball one day in gym class, and somebody intentionally tripped me.

They put their foot out, and I tripped. As a result, I flew into the wall and broke my arm, which hurt me severely. The worst part was that they weren't even apologetic about the fact that I got severely injured. Instead, they made fun of me for needing help with daily tasks as my hand had a cast. They would say, "Awww, your mommy had to dress you for school. Poor baby," among other things, to provoke me.

I got so fed up with all the bullying that one day, I left the school at the end of the day, hoping never to return. I walked the 10-mile home and told my parents I wanted to leave the technical school and return to my previous school to escape all that bullying. When the school principal and the guidance counselor learned about my decision to leave the school, they called me at home to reconsider my decision as they didn't want me to leave and assured me to take action against the bullying boys.

Then, along with my mother, I went to the school for an open conversation and told them upfront, "I am done with this school. I hate this school." I said, "I like the school and what it offers, but I don't like the people in it." So, I completed the rest of my school year at my previous school, where I studied for grades 7 and 8. Then, I went to high school with the entire class, which were great years. I made several new friends and got closer to the ones I already had.

High school was also the time when I started to drink more steadily. Although it wasn't my first time, as I had my first drink at a very young age, I started drinking more often in 10th grade. The first time I drank alcohol was with my father. I was 12 years old, and we had gone skiing, where he allowed me to have a few sips of his wine.

I was in the orchestra in the 11th grade when we had an opportunity to go to England and do concerts there, have a tour of the country, and play in the symphony halls of different places in England and Scotland. It was an extraordinary experience for me. It was a trip of a lifetime, especially for a kid who hadn't been overseas before. We played in halls over 200 years old and learned about the country's deep history of music and Arts.

Me and fellow students in the symphony orchestra

England's laws of alcohol consumption were way more lenient, and most of the kids with us could go out and legally drink. The pubs never asked us for IDs and had no qualms with serving alcohol to teenagers.

It was a surprising yet welcomed cultural shock for kids going from America. There we were, students ranging from 14-year-olds to 17-year-olds, in the pubs and drinking. We were all happy about that, and that trip was one of the reasons my high school years were the best years of my academic life.

In my senior year, I had enough credits that there was a time when I only had to take 1 class. I could get out of school every day at 10 a.m. I was able to start my first self-employed job during that time. As mentioned in an earlier chapter, I worked for my brother-in-law, Paul, and it was my first real job aside from some short-term jobs I had done over the years.

I got my driving license in grade 10. As I could drive, I went to work at Sears for a little while. I worked in paints and sporting goods.

One day, my mom called me, extremely concerned. She had gotten a call from the police, saying there was a robbery, and the getaway car had my license plates on it. I was mortified at the time. After repeatedly telling my mother I was at work, I ran outside to check my car and found my license plates missing. Someone had stolen my license plates and put them in another car to rob a gas station.

Thankfully, I didn't get in trouble as it wasn't my car, and my plates were obviously stolen. It was one of those weird things that happened to me as a teenager that I still think about. My childhood was filled with various events, some that still hurt to think about, but knowing that everything that happened in my life was for a reason. It all got me to this point, helped provide some solace, and put things into a positive perspective. My childhood's positive and negative aspects were all part of my journey, which I want to share with the world through this book.

Chapter 4: Getting Started

Alcohol has unknowingly been a focal point of my life and played a key part in shaping my life. Only recently, after getting rid of the constrictive hold it had on me, was I able to breathe freely after ages.

I was 12 when I first drank alcohol to the point where I could feel its effects. That was when I went skiing with my dad. My dad liked his wine, so he was drinking some after skiing, and I asked him if I could have a sip. My parents allowed me to sip alcohol occasionally in the privacy of our home. Maybe they wanted to remove children's intrigue towards anything they are denied.

My dad told me I could sip, and I had a few big gulps. I wanted to know the reason people seemed to love it so much. It made me feel a happy little buzz and made me sleepy. I slept for a long time afterward and loved how it made me feel.

The next memorable interaction that I had with alcohol was also with my dad when I was 14. I was building a garage with my dad at the lake house, and my dad, a beer lover, always brought it with him. After we were done with the work, I asked him if I could have a beer, and he let me have one of his beers as a reward for all my hard work.

I remember being in 10th grade when I first truly got drunk with a friend of mine in the neighborhood. I was 15 and randomly went to the house of a friend who lived up the street. He showed me a bottle of whisky and offered me some. It was my first time trying hard liquor.

To hide from his parents, we climbed out of his room on his roof, where he had a couple of bean bags placed, and started gulping down the hard alcohol, having no clue about moderation, how much we should drink, or what was too much. Everything seemed hilarious, and the world seemed like a big joke when we got drunk for the first time. We laughed and made conversation as we rapidly drank through the once-full bottle of whisky.

Afterward, when I tried getting back through the window, I felt like the walls were closing in on me as I tripped through the window opening. We got extremely clumsy in our drunken state as we laughed hysterically, and I tumbled down the staircase, which didn't even phase me.

I tried going to the bathroom, and I accidentally broke the toilet seat in my drunken stupor. I came out to his living room and attempted to sit down in their recliner chair. But I was so uncoordinated that as I leaned back, the chair tipped over backward and broke.

I felt embarrassed, but we laughed so hard that we soon forgot about everything. I then walked home, which was a few houses down. I didn't know how to hide my obvious stupor, so I tried pretending everything was normal when I got home.

My mom came up to me and said, "Oh good, you're home. I made some beef stew. Help yourself to some dinner."

I tried to hold it all in front of my mother and made it to the bathroom before completely losing control. I got what felt like deathly sick as I puked my guts out.

The unregulated and fast-paced consumption of whiskey was finally showing its effects on my body. I stayed cooped up in the bathroom for a while, and when I felt a little better, I came out and continued to pretend that everything was okay.

My mom was walking past me, and she said, "Oh God, what's that smell? It smells like whiskey."

It's true that you really can't hide anything from a mother.

A few days later, my father brought it up in passing, saying, *"I heard you had a little too much to drink the other day."*

I replied that I was still reaping its effects and didn't want to talk about it.

This made him laugh at my condition, and he replied, "*You live, and you learn.*"

I was so sick for the next couple of days after that reckless drinking that I vowed to myself that I would never drink again.

Sadly, It didn't take long until I started casually mixing hard alcohol with other beverages at home to seek the buzz from alcohol. I would mix some hard alcohol with some orange juice and have a couple of such drinks before going to school. I would be on the school bus feeling the alcoholic high, giggling to myself, while everyone else was unaware of my little secret. Feeling the alcohol wear off was never a good experience; it wore off and turned into a headache and a light hangover.

Then came the once-in-a-lifetime school trip to Europe, which gave me the confidence to drink openly in public with my peers for the first time. Most of us would spend the nights in pubs, some drinking out of control. After getting my license and first car, I grew increasingly bold in my alcohol consumption. I would pick up friends on the way to school and sometimes bring a couple of beers in the car with me to share before school. It wasn't a daily routine, but it happened too often.

Some days, my friends and I would go to someone's house, sneak a couple of beers in, and drink them, feeling like true rebels chasing our high. In high school, I would often go up to the lakehouse with my friends and pick up beers along the way. I was always nervous about buying alcohol underage but almost always got away with it.

I would sneak some of my dad's beers, and some of my neighbors at the lake house, who were also around my age, would sneak hard liquor from their parents' stash, and we would share and drink together when our parents weren't around. I would hide beers under towels to go party on the lake by boat. We would then sink the empty bottles and cans by filling them with water to avoid being caught with empty cans of alcohol. I didn't want to deal with what my parents might say and think. Even though they weren't strict, I preferred not to be obvious.

My parents weren't strictly against my alcohol consumption. They only wanted me to restrict it to inside the home. In fact, there was a time in my late teens that they would buy beers for me.

The lakehouse was also where I got extremely drunk for the second time in my life, making me vow never to drink excessively again. I was drinking with neighbor friends at the lake house, drinking my father's beer and the alcohol they provided, and it got to a point where my head started to spin. I was young and naive and had no idea about how much to drink and how to regulate my drinking. I just wanted to drink, and I soon started getting the feeling of drinking too much. I tried lying down to alleviate my spinning head, but the room kept spinning, and I ended up throwing up all night.

I once again promised myself that I would never do this again. This put me on another one of my temporary alcohol cleanses, which would last for a couple of months but never got up to a year.

After getting my first car, I would pick up a couple of friends, go to neighboring states where the alcohol consumption age was 18, and drink legally. We would go up to Vermont or Connecticut while living in Massachusetts. We would drive all the way there, go to a bar, get lots of drinks and food, and drive home a hundred miles away. We would drive such long distances under the influence and always get away with it.

One time, when I was 18, I was driving my new car with a friend who drank with me. We were going across town in my car to pick up another friend, and I had beers in the car, and we had been drinking them. As I came to the town center, a roadblock and detour were set up, with a police car blocking the main road.

As I got to the roadblock, I freaked out. I sped through the roadblock, not knowing my plan of action. I saw the cop running toward us, and my friend and I started throwing beer bottles out of the window, trying to get rid of any evidence. Seeing me speed up, the cop thought I was making a run for it and called for backup, while in reality, I was just being stupid as I had no clue how to deal with such a situation. As I went around the bend, I realized the reason for the roadblock: a church was ablaze. I was internally freaking out, thinking that I would definitely go to jail for this. We threw away every beer bottle we could get our hands on, whether empty or full.

Finally, two cop cars pulled me over, and I made the excuse that I wasn't paying attention and didn't notice the barricade, so I didn't stop. I told them that I go through this route every day, and I was driving on autopilot. I thought they were looking for speeding cars when I saw a cop car.

After I gave my lousy explanation, the cops exchanged glances as if they were telling each other that we could nail these kids today and teach them a lesson they'll never forget.

I was internally freaking out as they went back to verify my license and told my friend not to screw this up any further for me. My friend was from my neighborhood and notorious for not liking the cops and stirring up all types of trouble. The same kid I got drunk with on his roof. Thankfully, he had enough mind to stay quiet, and as the cops came back, all I could think was I would get arrested today.

The cop returned my license and registration and said, "Just go where you're going, and don't go anywhere from there. Get rid of the beers that are in your car."

And I was sitting there, dumbfounded that I might be arrested today. "*What beers?*" I asked naively, thinking I was smug in my hiding tactics.

"There are two beers on your back seat," he replied matter-of-factly.

"Oh yeah, those, I'll get rid of them, officer," I played it off casually.

Later on, I couldn't believe that he not only let me go but even let me leave with beers in the back seat. Thinking back, I believe that if I had gotten a DUI that day, it would have completely altered the course of my life.

Another encounter with law enforcement that I think would've changed my life had it resulted in a different outcome happened when I was 20. I had recently turned 20, and it was the legal drinking age at the time in Massachusetts. I was drinking with my friends, and we started getting those Long Island iced teas with eight combined liquors.

I had several of those that night and drove my friend home in my new car. I dropped him off and was returning home when it started raining. I was only a few miles from home, and my car was fast. It was a

Honda CRX, like a sports car at the time. I was speeding my way home when I saw a car approaching me at a bend. I lost control of my car due to the wet roads, combined with my inebriated state, and my car spun and crashed into a tree and then into an oncoming car.

I remember thinking to myself, "You are so screwed. There is no way you can get out of this. They will be able to smell the alcohol on you."

Thankfully, no one was seriously injured. One of the passengers in the other car broke their nose, but nothing life-threatening. Both cars were completely totaled, and I had a gash on my forehead. I remember getting out of the car, thinking my life was over.

The only thing the cop asked me when he saw me was, *"Where are your shoes?"*

My shoes had gotten stuck under the dashboard, and I was walking in my socks on a wet road with glass scattered all over it. I was so caught up in shock that I didn't feel anything due to the adrenaline rush after the accident. The cops told me to go in the ambulance to get my wounds checked out, and I was transported to the hospital. Neither the cops nor the nurses even questioned me about my drinking.

It was a big moment in my life, as someone could've gotten seriously injured because of my careless decision to drive under the influence. It acted as a wake-up call, and I intentionally stopped drinking for a while again. I now have the insight to know that I should have stopped completely. It was what I needed, but it didn't take long before I was drinking again, although I avoided drinking and driving for a long time as my drinking became a bigger problem while my depression and anxiety increased.

Chapter 5: Attempts to Break the Cycle

My dependency on alcohol as a coping mechanism started when the bullying began in junior high school. I would turn to alcohol to take the edge off of the depression and anxiety. After realizing my problems, I recognized my need to stay busy to keep myself distracted, so I started exploring other activities to stay busy and sober.

I wasn't rich by any means and didn't have thousands of dollars lying around to pursue every activity, but I heard some talks about scuba diving, and it had been a dream of mine to do that from childhood, as a young kid swimming in the lake. So I signed up for the classes with some friends, became PADI certified, bought equipment, and became healthy and addicted to a new and amazing activity.

Although I started diving for adventure and to regulate my depression and drinking, we always ended the day with a cooler full of ice-cold beer. We would have fun diving. We would catch lobsters and have a party at the beachside, and I would drink too, but I made efforts to drink moderately, wanting to minimize my secret problem.

As time passed, I wanted to pursue my other big passion, skydiving, which always sounded thrilling to me. I was trying to chase every form of adrenaline at that point in my life to overcome the depression that never seemed to go away.

I was terrified the first time I went skydiving, especially when the door opened. My mind went numb. Overwhelming fear and excitement at the same time. When I was told to jump, I said, "Who, me?"

During my first attempt at skydiving,

When I jumped, I couldn't think of anything other than what was happening at the moment. For the first time in my life, I had found something that totally consumed my thoughts, and my depression literally disappeared. I wasn't thinking about drinking, I wasn't depressed, and I wasn't even worried about the future. In those few moments, my mind was truly at peace, and it provided me with the most blissful feeling of my life. I was feeling scared yet excited, and that was all I felt. I instantly craved more.

When I landed a stand-up landing, it seemed unreal that jumping out of an airplane, steering a parachute to the ground, and landing like stepping down a step could make me feel these indescribable feelings and emotions. For the first time in my adult life, I got to experience intense excitement without the help of alcohol or drugs.

However, now I had a new addiction...Adrenaline. I started chasing that feeling the very next day, and within my first year of skydiving, I did close to 400 jumps and started my new career as a Tandem, Static line, free-fall instructor, and pilot soon after.

While attempting free-fall

The skydiving kept me busy, and I stopped drinking during the day, but at night, after the skydiving was done, we would crack open the beer and wine to end the day and begin the night activities.

It was all part of the experience. We would celebrate the great day of jumping by drinking beer and smoking joints around the campfire while reminiscing the dives of the day.

Before then, I hadn't been a big fan of pot. I had tried it before during my teenage years but didn't like how it made me feel. I felt like its effects lasted too long, and when I did it inside, I felt as though the walls were closing in on me.

With every skydiving "first" came the drop zone rule of buying a case of beer to share. First water jump, first-night jump, first nude jump, etc. Some weekends, I had to buy multiple cases. There was almost never a lack of beer.

Skydiving helped open up various opportunities for me. I did a sponsored demo jump in Texas, carrying the banner flag of AT&T at a Willy Nelson concert. I was under the influence of crystal meth. I knew what I was doing was dangerous and careless, but I did it anyway.

Drinking wasn't allowed during jumping operations, but unofficially, sometimes rules were bent a little. The last load of the day was known as the

Sunset load because you were jumping at sunset. It became almost a ritual to bring a beer or two on the plane hidden inside our jumpsuits and drink it on the way up to 13,000 feet as long as there were no students on board. I didn't know about it at first, but it sure became fun, and I always looked forward to the sunset load.

I remember thinking, "Oh, so this is what you guys do on sunset load!"

We would crush the empty beer cans and bring them down in our jumpsuits, and proceed to drink more and party the night away once we landed.

I remember going up to 12,000 feet with friends on a hot day, jumping out of the plane, opening the parachute right away, drinking a can of beer while flying around in the clouds, enjoying the cool air, and landing off-field somewhere.

I still remember the blissful feeling of getting the buzz of the alcohol on top of the buzz I got from the adrenaline rush of every jump. The combination of adrenaline and alcohol plus the lack of oxygen at high altitudes hugely magnified the effects.

As much as I loved skydiving, the negative effects of the extracurricular activities weren't so good. The drinking and partying and the drugs, although bad for my health, were fun and exhilarating for a while and some of the best times of my life. That was also around the time when I met my wife. There were many times that I attempted to stop or cut back on the substances, but the drugs and especially the booze eventually caught up to me. I couldn't get up in the morning and was not motivated to go to work, causing my business to dwindle and causing further financial problems in my life.

I now recognize that my relationship with my wife became tainted due to alcohol. We enjoyed drinking, and we went through times of drinking every night. It was a regular part of our relationship.

I was also into smoking pot at the time. Many times, she told me that I shouldn't be smoking or drinking so much; it might be harmful. So, I agreed but later continued it behind her back.

I couldn't stop myself, and there were a couple of times when she would get suspicious and say, "*I smell pot. Did you smoke pot?*"

I would almost always deny it, not wanting her to judge me for my vices. I believe that my lying caused a crack in our relationship that we could never mend, and it kept growing.

Somewhere in the mix, years later, I was involved in another car accident, which acted as another wake-up call. It happened on my way back from work one day. I picked up a 16-ounce beer and some chips on my way back from my day job and was drinking while on my way home when the accident occurred. It had become a daily occurrence to pick up a beer on my way home from work.

The accident wasn't my fault this time, but I had the beer can open in my car, which spilled all over me when I crashed, leaving me soaked with beer.

I got out to assess the situation, and luckily, no one was hurt.

One person who witnessed the accident whispered in my ear, "*Have you been drinking?*" he could smell the alcohol on me.

I was extremely embarrassed and said, "*Yeah, I just opened a beer in the truck.*"

It went completely silent after that, and no one said anything to me. Although I didn't get into any legal trouble, I stopped drinking and driving from that day onward.

I tried not to drink and drive more seriously than ever before in my life. I did not drive under the influence for about twenty years after that incident. Even though I drank nearly every day, I never dared to go behind the wheel under the influence to endanger the lives of innocent people, including my own and risked my license.

The drugs and especially the booze eventually caught up to me. I couldn't get up in the morning and was not motivated to go to work, causing my business to dwindle and causing further financial problems in my life.

Although my intentions were to stop or at least cut back on drinking and drugs, it always crept back in damaging ways.

Chapter 6: Starting a Business

I have lived a fulfilling and exciting life, and although my career choices have worked for me, looking back, I wish I had done things differently. I have always had a passion for weather and flying. I believe that if I had pursued those passions and explored the science of meteorology and commercial flight, I might have found a more truly satisfying full-time career.

While we've talked about my part-time career as a skydiving instructor and pilot, a significant chapter of my life remains untold—the cornerstone of my livelihood and my eventual downfall.

As I mentioned in one of the previous chapters, my first full-time job was with Paul, my brother-in-law. I would get out of school by ten and work for him during my last year of high school. Working with Paul enriched my knowledge and taught me the skills required to do the window tinting business, which I continued doing for over 30 years. As a young individual eager to step into the world, I expanded into commercial, residential, and security window films as I began to move away from cars.

Over time, after buying a home, I decided to start a real estate business, purchasing, renovating, renting, and selling multi-family homes.

I was a subcontractor while working with Paul and installed accessories on cars, such as sunroofs, pinstriping, body moldings, roof racks, and spoilers. At 18 years old, it seemed like a dream job, getting to spend most of my day surrounded by cars and working to make them look beautiful. That business slowly evolved, and it was my sole source of income at one point in time.

My adrenaline-seeking mind sought new adventures often, yet I never gave up on my business and continued expanding and working on it while indulging in exciting activities after work. With time, my business grew steadily, and I got to reap the benefits of the years of hard work I put into it, as well as free time to enjoy my passions.

I started focusing on my business more than ever before when my then-girlfriend and I decided to get married. We wanted to ensure we had enough savings to buy a house before we got married, so my wife and I started working hard to sell our services as she continued her career path in accounting.

The perks of a service-based business are that your sales are determined by how well and smoothly you can sell what you have to offer, combined with good quality work to encourage people to buy your services. So, my wife and I started promoting our car accessory business by doing a lot of footwork and cold-calling.

We were young people, excited at the prospect of new beginnings and being a homeowner. We would go to car dealerships, hoping for bulk orders, informing them of our services, and trying to convince them that they could make extra money selling our products and services to their customers.

In 1993, after five years together, we bought our first house. We lived there for five years when we had our first daughter, Madison, and found another beautiful house that we purchased in 1999. With the quickly rising real estate prices, I started to get serious about starting my real estate business. We bought a fixer-upper two-family house in 2002, and its value in the market rose quickly when we rented it within the first few years after renovating it. I was thrilled by the discovery and quickly found our next project, a three-family home, and did the same thing with the money we made from the first rental property. The concept was to continue the process of buying, fixing, renting, and selling.

Our first two homes, New Hampshire

My first rental property

My second rental property

The business van at home

I tried to do as much of the renovation on my own as possible. I would only hire professionals to do things I didn't know how to do, like the roofing, plumbing, and electrical parts of the buildings, trying to make as big of a profit as possible.

Knowing my way around tools helped me successfully as I learned a lot. Some of the learning was painful. This extensive process entailed meeting legal requirements, ensuring the properties were fit for occupancy, and finding suitable tenants.

Although this business was not devoid of risks, I achieved notable success with my initial property, reaping substantial profits.

However, not every aspect unfolded according to plan. In the second property, I had to do lots of extra expensive work that I wasn't expecting. A staircase had to be installed on the third floor to make it legal. The cost was $20,000, which I had to borrow.

That was when the crash of the real estate market of 2008 happened, leaving me in significant debt, with no possible way of turning my gamble on the house into a profit.

The house value dropped below what I owed. Most of my money was tied up in a bad asset. It took 12 stressful years of my life until I eventually was able to sell it at break-even.

I felt as though I was dealing with crises left and right. Not only was I not able to profit from my most recent house, but I also had to deal with challenging tenants who seemingly held more rights than landlords. I had some great tenants, too, but evicting the bad ones became an arduous task, as evicting disruptive tenants became an uphill and expensive battle.

The mounting stress and pressure exacted their toll on me, giving rise to heightened anxiety and depression. Balancing the demands of managing the real estate business, maintaining properties, handling tenants, and fulfilling familial responsibilities, as well as my other business, became an overwhelming juggling act, ultimately contributing to my eventual collapse.

Another big financial hit I faced around the same time as the real estate collapse was losing my biggest car tinting client. I was employed by a limousine manufacturer, the country's third-largest manufacturer. I did the window tints of every one of their cars that were built there.

The work was year-round, and I worked with them for around 17 years. I had grown tired of the repetitive nature of the work and the bad-tempered foreman, craving something different.

I didn't want to quit the job as it was a cheque that played an important role in making ends meet, but I couldn't take the arrogant anger from the foreman anymore. One day, while involved in a heated, senseless argument, I quit on the spot. Although it provided temporary relief from a management perspective, it also caused a big financial blow at a time when I was already struggling.

I had relied on that income for years, and not having it when I was already facing financial stability hit me harder than I had thought. I was increasingly concerned about our financial situation, fearing bankruptcy. But, like always, we struggled through it, and we persevered. Uncertainty became a constant part of my life.

However, in the face of these hurdles, I persisted, seizing the opportunities that presented themselves. I started to focus once again on my window tinting job. I wanted to persevere and get my family out of this financial situation we had landed in after the real estate business collapsed. Never one to turn down a job, I consistently went the extra mile, trying to fulfill customers' requests and deliver exceptional service.

During those turbulent times, hope arose when I secured work in Texas, where I completed a project at a Grand Hyatt in San Antonio. It wasn't a huge job, but it was a custom decorative film job that helped us make it through that winter.

My wife and I made it a working mini vacation. It was a great feeling doing work at a national level. I also gained jobs at many Rite-Aids throughout New England and New York for a few years, thanks to several contractors who found my website and awarded me the jobs.

My all-time biggest job came from winning a bid at Manchester-Boston regional airport, where I tinted several hundred terminal windows. The job was so big that I had to hire several guys and ask various friends to help with the project.

However, beneath the surface of these positive experiences, the persistent undercurrent of anxiety and depression persisted, magnified by the weight of managing numerous responsibilities and the constant fear of failure. Some individuals unwaveringly stood by my side throughout my journey, offering consistent support and invaluable guidance. My wife, in particular, played a pivotal role in the smooth operation of our businesses, deftly handling accounting and sales. Together, we formed a formidable team until the weight of my personal struggles began to overshadow our partnership.

Marital problems and the gradual deterioration of our relationship mirrored the decline of my mental and emotional well-being. Recognizing the need for assistance, I sought professional counselling and received medication to alleviate my anxiety and depression.

I succumbed to the trap of addiction, seeking solace in alcohol as a coping mechanism for mounting pressures. The ensuing cycle of addiction wrought devastation, breeding deceit and lies. I unwittingly sacrificed my most cherished relationship for the temporary respite that alcohol seemed to offer. My marriage struggled as the astonishing power of addiction revealed itself, eroding my business ventures and the bonds I held dear.

In hindsight, I recognize the profound emotional toll accompanying my financial and career pursuits. The mounting stress, anxiety, and depression gradually exacerbated my challenges. Addiction greatly intensified these struggles, eroding everything.

Yet, despite the hardships, I carry few regrets about my life and believe that each experience, whether it brought joy or pain, has shaped me into the individual I am today. I have learned valuable lessons about the essence of perseverance, self-awareness, determination, and the importance of seeking support when navigating life's complexities. The road ahead remains uncertain as my journey continues and evolves, but I face it with unyielding resilience, determined to rebuild and rediscover the true meaning of fulfillment.

Chapter 7: Love

Throughout my life, the yearning for love and meaningful relationships burned within me like a flickering flame. It was a deep-seated desire to find that elusive soul who would complete me, to discover a connection that transcended the ordinary.

But whenever the possibility of a potential relationship shimmered on the horizon, a torrent of emotions engulfed me, leaving me trembling with nerves, unable to take the plunge. The mere thought of shouldering the responsibilities that came with commitment instilled a sense of overwhelming anxiety, making me recoil from the prospect. In those tender years of adolescence, whenever a budding connection hinted at the possibility of blossoming into something significant, I found myself feeling utterly unprepared and ill-equipped to navigate the complexities of love.

Dark clouds of doubt loomed over my mind, casting shadows on any flicker of hope. My thoughts became a swirling vortex of apprehension, conjuring up potential failure and heartbreak scenarios. The weight of my insecurities eclipsed any glimmer of optimism, rendering me blind to the beauty that could emerge from such connections. In those moments before I met my wife, I had made myself believe that the threads of destiny would never weave a tapestry of profound connection for me. I had surrendered to the notion that marriage was destined to elude my grasp, forever out of reach.

Me with the love of my life, 1989

But fate had other plans, and on that fateful summer, when our paths intersected, my world was irrevocably altered. At that point in my life, I was a couple of years into my skydiving journey, focused solely on the adrenaline rush I would get from the jump. The notion of love and romance had been neatly tucked away, locked in a hidden chamber of my heart.

Like a shooting star streaking across the night sky, she appeared intent on learning the art of defying gravity. Our initial encounters sparked conversations that effortlessly flowed, weaving a tapestry of shared interests and heartfelt confessions. A genuine friendship flourished; each moment spent together nurturing the seeds of an unspoken connection.

As time passed, our bond deepened, and the boundaries of friendship expanded to envelop the realm of romance. She became not just a friend but a beacon of light in the stormy seas of my emotions. She became my girlfriend, and the significance of that title reverberated through the chambers of my heart.

Our love language was doing acts of service for each other. I truly believed she loved me when she volunteered to be my first tandem passenger to gain my tandem skydive instructor rating, which turned out to be my most frightening jump as an uncontrollable spin developed while in free-fall. Our falling bodies, hooked together, began to spin like a propeller, and I couldn't stop it. I pulled the ripcord as the examiner slowed my spin by pushing my legs.

We landed safely, but the memory of that intense adrenaline during those few seconds still stays with me. Although we barely escaped an accident, she was still willing and happy to continue practicing with me on the following examined jumps to complete my certification.

The flames of shared adventure and mutual exhilaration drew us closer together. And so, we decided to establish our humble abode in an older 22-

foot camping trailer at the airport's drop zone, where we shared our love for the daring sport that had initially brought us together.

Our trailer enhanced our joy of camping and adventure. Living together successfully in a small trailer helped to grow us even closer together, knowing that if we could co-exist in a cramped space, we could live anywhere together, which grew our excitement and hopes of traveling the world.

As the winter chill descended upon us, we were offered a temporary home for the winter. We moved into the drop zone owners' home located on the property. We took care of things, including plowing, and arranged occasional jumping on the cold weekends in exchange for very low rent. It was a place where warmth replaced the biting cold of the season, offering respite from the frigid winds of Maine that howled outside. Friends would stop by, and we enjoyed a warm fire and cocktails.

We watched National Park documentaries as our minds became consumed with thoughts of embarking on the grand journey together, and we diligently worked towards saving money for this dream road trip. The apartment walls were witness to our relentless determination as we scoured every corner of our budget, saving money in pursuit of this shared aspiration.

Our hearts remained restless, yearning for adventure and the allure of distant lands. Alaska beckoned to us, its rugged landscapes and untamed beauty calling out. Our minds became consumed with thoughts of embarking on this grand journey together, and we diligently worked towards accumulating the money required to turn this dream into a reality.

We lived back and forth between the trailer and apartments for a couple of years. We would spend our free time visiting Lake Winnipesaukee and Vermont and seeing our parents. Hiking, cycling, skiing, and eventually flying were part of our routines, as well as with friends.

Lake Winnipesaukee my favorite place on Earth

We formed a great friendship with Glenn, a skydiver who was also an adventurer. We all became so close that he was the Best Man at our wedding years later. I also earned my Private Pilot license, and we would fly to different parts of New England for breakfast and lunch or just to see the beauty from a bird's eye view. My love of flying continues today in the form of soaring in a glider, which began at age 14. My mom sparked my interest in flying while I began glider lessons as she did.

Within our home, we engaged in heartfelt conversations and allowed time to weave its magic. Our love story was not a hurried sprint but a steady journey of self-discovery and mutual understanding. Each passing day brought us closer, strengthening the bond that held us together. As the doubts dissipated, I began to see the unwavering love and commitment that resided within her. She became my missing link, leading me toward a future of forever love and companionship.

Amidst the practicalities of apartment hunting and saving, a whisper emerged—a desire to own a place we could call our own. The notion of stability tugged at the edges of our dreams, intertwining with the allure of travel.

And so, we embarked on a journey to find a house that could serve as the anchor for our love while still accommodating our nomadic spirits. During this time, we stumbled upon a camper van—a symbol of freedom and wanderlust. It was a serendipitous find, arriving just before the seeds of homeownership began to take root in our minds.

With the camper van in our possession, we set off on our first grand adventure, steering our wheels southward toward the enchanting shores of Key West, Florida. Along the way, we relished the thrill of skydiving, infusing each pit stop with exhilaration and laughter. Campgrounds became our temporary havens, where we parked our van and shared stories around crackling campfires, our spirits soaring high. The memory of those sun-kissed days, filled with a heavy mix of adrenaline and wanderlust, became etched in the very fabric of our shared history and future.

Yet, as with any grand expedition, the journey was not without its trials. As the miles stretched beneath our wheels, the reality of financial constraints began to grow.

Once filled with promise and endless horizons, the road became a stark reminder of our limited resources. In Key West, our pockets emptied, we maxed out a credit card and had to borrow gas money to return home, but we embraced the unpredictability of our adventures. We were adventurers embracing the unpredictable yet always cognizant of the balance between dreams and practicality.

Amid our whirlwind escapades, doubts crept into my mind, mirroring the cautionary tales of my own family. The scars left by my sibling's divorce etched themselves into my memory, cautioning me to tread carefully when it came to matters of the heart. I yearned to ensure that my partner was truly the one with whom I could weather the storms of life and avoid the painful paths walked by my sisters. The weight of this decision pressed upon me, demanding patience and introspection.

As our lives together blossomed, we engaged in heartfelt conversations and allowed time to weave its magic. Our love story was not a hurried sprint but a steady journey of self-discovery and mutual understanding. Each passing day brought us closer, strengthening the bond that held us together. And as the doubts dissipated, I began to see the unwavering love and commitment that resided within her. She proved to be the guiding light, illuminating the path toward a future where the pain of divorce would remain a distant specter.

In the midst of uncertainty, we clung to hope and perseverance. Our home became a sanctuary for introspection, where love and pragmatism danced a delicate waltz. And over time, I realized she was the one, the partner whose steadfast presence could withstand the trials of life.

Chapter 8: Marriage

After being together for five years and buying a house, we both knew how deeply we valued each other and our relationship. Although I knew the next step of our relationship was to get married, bringing up the conversation wasn't exactly as simple as that. The seed had been sown in the crisp days of fall, perhaps September or October, a time of transition much like our relationship. The idea had quietly taken root, nurtured by silent contemplation over time, until it flourished into something more substantial.

I gained the courage to start talking about the next step, wanting to gauge if we were on the same frequency. She agreed that we would eventually get married, leaving the conversation hanging.

The ball was now in my court, and I knew it was up to me to progress the situation. So, with what little money I had in savings, I went to the jewelers. I can still feel the anticipation that tugged at my heartstrings, the fluttering uncertainty accompanying a significant step. The engagement ring I held felt weighty with promise, even if it wasn't as extravagant as I believed she deserved. I knew our bond was strong enough that the size of the ring would not matter to her. Financial constraints led me to a modest yet heartfelt choice, reflecting my sincere intentions.

And so, in a moment that felt surreal and profoundly real, I simply offered her the gift that held my hopes and dreams. I acted as casually as possible, with my heart on my sleeve. Nestled within a small box, wrapped in anticipation, the ring symbolized a future we had glanced at only in our conversations. As the lid lifted, revealing the embodiment of my love and commitment, she started softly crying tears of joy.

The words that tumbled from my lips were far from rehearsed or elegant, yet they carried the weight of a thousand promises. "I was thinking we could maybe get married soon." The vulnerability in that statement hung in the air, a shared vulnerability that now bound us even tighter.

Her response, a repeated "Yes, of course," reverberated within the cozy confines of our apartment. It wasn't a grand, orchestrated event, nor did it involve the traditional bended knee. But it was perfect in its own right, an unscripted act filled with emotions.

Looking back, I wish I had done something more romantic to express my love, but the authenticity of that moment remains untouched. It was a testament to us, the love that had matured over years of togetherness and the unspoken understanding that made words almost redundant.

And so, in the quiet embrace of our shared space, we set forth on a new chapter, our hearts brimming with anticipation and joy. Her wedding ring was custom-made by one of our friends, Al, who was a talented jeweler.

Several months after our engagement, we stumbled upon a house that we decided to lay our roots in and purchase, putting all of our focus on this endeavor. In preparation for the biggest investment of our lives towards our relationship, we had to sell our van, anticipating the possibility of obtaining another one later down the line. This moment marked a significant and thrilling milestone in our lives.

I vividly remember the day when the house deal was finalized. We commemorated the occasion by toasting with a bottle of champagne, signifying the beginning of our new life as homeowners. Despite not being married yet, possessing the house made us feel like a married couple, embracing genuine responsibilities such as maintenance and yard work to make it our own.

We resided in that house for a total of five years, a period of substantial growth for us. We confronted life's challenges hand-in-hand, and our experiences as homeowners eased the notion of marriage, making it feel less daunting and more familiar.

During our first winter in the house, we faced many challenges, like a leaking roof and a broken furnace. It was a big eye-opener for us about the realities of home ownership. Despite the difficulties, we built a two-story, two-car garage during our time there.

In 1993, towards the end of our first winter at our house, we embarked on an unforgettable ski trip. We headed out West to Colorado for a week of deep snow winter skiing. Then, we continued to Lake Tahoe for another week, enjoying California and Nevada's deep snow and springtime conditions. It was truly a fantastic and memorable adventure.

When we returned from the trip, some friends and family jokingly asked if we had eloped and gotten married during our vacation. The idea surprised me, and for a moment, I thought it would be a wonderful thing to do. We were engaged then but hadn't set a concrete plan or date for the wedding. It was around the end of March or the beginning of April 1993.

With that thought in our minds, we both realized that we loved the idea of winter weddings and couldn't wait another year to get married. To avoid waiting another year, we took matters into our own hands and organized the wedding within four weeks of returning from our two-week skiing vacation. We planned and executed everything ourselves, fully immersing ourselves in the experience while enjoying each other's company.

We were both surprised by our friends who planned a bachelor/bachelorette event for each of us. Glenn hired a limousine for me and the guys. They took me to a strip club. I felt uncomfortable, but it was all innocent, and we had fun. I joked with Glenn that he needed it more than I did. The ladies took Judy by limo to a nice restaurant with gifts.

Our ceremony and reception took place at the Governer's Inn in Rochester, New Hampshire, and around 100 friends and family joined us for this unforgettable and joyous occasion.

The feedback from our guests was overwhelming, with many of them remarking that it was the best wedding they had ever attended, brimming with fun and laughter. While a traditional honeymoon wasn't within our budget, we viewed our two-week ski vacation as our pre-marriage honeymoon. Additionally, we enjoyed a long weekend together, although our initial plans for skiing had to be altered due to the closing of the slopes at Sugarloaf in Maine.

Despite the unexpected change, we made the most of it by heading to the beautiful coast of Maine near Booth Bay Harbor, where we spent a relaxing night, cherishing the beginning of our life together as a confirmed couple. Following this memorable time, we embarked on a new venture by expanding our business, focusing on window tinting and automotive work. I left my brother-in-law's support and ventured into this endeavor with Judy by my side, determined to build a successful and fulfilling life together.

Taking full ownership of the business was a significant and somewhat scary moment for us. After buying the house, we found ourselves with just $900 left to our name, which made us feel nervous and excited about the future. It was a big step, and we were aware of the responsibilities that came with it.

I focused intensely on growing the business, feeling determined to succeed. Though we weren't wealthy, we managed to find joy in our lives. I continued my passions for skiing and skydiving, even though I gradually stopped instructing due to the stress it brought, knowing that lives depended on my decisions during jumps.

As time went on, we found a balance in life. I concentrated on the business while my wife pursued her degree in accounting, a step towards building a more secure future together. It was a time of hard work and shared dreams and aspirations, binding us together on this journey of life and love.

In January 1997, our blissful married life took an unexpected yet welcomed turn when Judy excitedly and surprisingly revealed that she was pregnant. Despite not planning to start a family immediately due to her recent graduation and job search, we embraced the surprise.

Brimming with nesting instincts, Judy prepared for the baby's arrival by organizing and painting the house. To ensure her safety, we hired assistance for the painting. Although I wasn't overly concerned about beautifying our house, I gave in to her demands, and she spent her days decorating our house for our new bundle of joy.

One workday, I received an anxious voicemail from Judy, stating that she wasn't feeling her best and was going to the hospital. Fearing the worst, I immediately rushed there despite the hour-and-a-half distance. To my surprise, upon arriving, I found my wife already in labor, with our baby's head making its entrance.

Worries about Judy's fear of labor pain and the hope for an epidural were in our minds, but it was too late. She endured the labor without painkillers. Our daughter's early arrival, five weeks ahead of schedule, added to the intensity and unexpectedness of the experience. Witnessing the birth was a profoundly spiritual and surreal moment, leaving me with a newfound appreciation for the miracle of life. I still get goosebumps when I think about that day when a new life was created.

Us, with our first-born, Madison

When our daughter entered the world, she cried, filling us with overwhelming joy. After the whirlwind of emotions subsided, we looked at each other, filled with wonder, shock, and gratitude for the extraordinary day we had shared.

Back then, communication lacked the instantaneous nature it has now, and nobody knew about the birth. Nevertheless, the memory of that momentous day will forever remain etched in our hearts, marking the beginning of a new chapter as we embraced parenthood and the unconditional love that came with it.

After Madison Brooke's arrival, we were eager to share the exciting news with our friends and family. When I called my dad from the hospital, he was keen to know the baby's gender, assuming we were revealing it, but the surprise was that our baby girl was already born! I could sense his tears of joy.

During our early days in the hospital, we experienced mixed emotions. Our daughter had difficulty latching on to breastfeeding, resulting in a readiness score of 8 for going home.

To ensure we could take her home, we needed to demonstrate her ability to feed comfortably. We spent five days at the hospital, trying various ways to help her feed comfortably. Though challenging, the hospital staff ingeniously devised a method involving my pinky finger, which we used to feed her, which enabled us to bring her home.

The first night at home with our baby girl was intense and overwhelming. Parenthood's challenges exceeded our expectations, with sleepless nights, constant feeding, and soothing a crying baby. We took turns caring for her, but there were no breaks.

As weeks passed, we gradually adjusted to our roles as parents, as our daughter started sleeping through the night, making things somewhat easier. However, the responsibility of being new parents remained a constant presence in our lives, and we embraced it with love and determination. Around this time, moving to a new place began to cross our minds. With our family growing, we wanted a fresh start in a new home where we could create more beautiful memories together. The decision to move brought both excitement and nervousness, signifying a new chapter in our lives filled with love, laughter, and the joys of parenthood.

We realized we wanted the new house closer to our family and friends and in an area with amenities like grocery stores and better healthcare options. The decision to sell our current house was emotional, considering the fond memories we had built there over the past five years. But we were eager for a fresh start and more convenience.

Thankfully, our house sold quickly, and we even profited from it. Simultaneously, we found a beautiful house about an hour away in Hampstead, New Hampshire. The neighborhood was unlike anything we had imagined living in, with doctors and professionals as our neighbors. It felt like a significant step up for us, an achievement in our journey.

Even though we knew we were far from the pinnacle of success, it was a major milestone in our eyes. The house's grandeur amazed us, and we were excited and grateful for the opportunity to call it our new home. After our first child was born, Judy began expressing her desire for a second child. She believed it was essential for our firstborn to have a sibling and grow up with a companion. While initially feeling a bit reluctant, I understood her perspective and eventually agreed, knowing it would enrich our family's journey. The idea of our family growing with love and togetherness brought warmth to our hearts, making us eager to embrace the future.

Nearly a year after our first child's birth, our family embraced the idea of welcoming a second child. Despite planning for this moment, Judy's pregnancy news filled us with delight as we looked forward to expanding our family.

Judy couldn't contain her excitement when she took a home pregnancy test and shared the positive results with me. Promptly, we scheduled a doctor's appointment, only to discover that Judy was already halfway through her pregnancy. We were astonished, reflecting on when we mistook morning sickness for the flu!

The days leading up to our daughter's birth felt like a whirlwind of anticipation, and she arrived a few weeks ahead of schedule, which seemed like perfect timing.

The night of her birth is etched in my memory. Around midnight, Judy got up, and upon her return, her water broke, causing us to panic. We rushed to the hospital at one o'clock in the morning, but we were pulled over by a rude cop for speeding, as we were going 35MPh in a 30MPh zone. He was extremely rude, and although he eventually let us go after unwarranted bickering and advice to 'call an ambulance next time,' the encounter added unexpected stress to an already nerve-wracking moment. His behavior was so uncalled for that I still get angry, remembering it 23 years later.

At the hospital, we learned Jacie Kendall was still in a breach position. Previous tests were done to assess the possibility of a natural birth. Despite preparing for a cesarean section, the medical team proceeded with a natural birth, ensuring Jacie's safe and healthy arrival.

The excitement and nervousness peaked as we felt blessed to welcome our second child into the world. The anticipation and surprise of her arrival made her birth even more miraculous, and the love and joy that enveloped us that night are forever etched in our hearts.

As Judy received the epidural, the tense atmosphere in the delivery room filled me with anxiety. As instructed, I held her body still for support, trying my best not to move. The moment of delivery was overwhelming and emotional. Jacie didn't come out head first; instead, her tiny rear end appeared first, followed by a leg, and then the other. It was a unique and surprising sight, but our hearts swelled joyfully when she finally emerged, crying and healthy. The surrounding staff of nurses and the doctor all had tears of joy at the safe arrival of our bundle of joy. The delivery left Jacie with bruises from the pressure, but overall, she was fine. Witnessing her birth was a miraculous experience, reminding me of the incredible journey of bringing new life into the world.

Some friends had assured us that having a second child would be easier than the first, but it proved challenging. Jacie cried more than her older sister, Madison. However, we embraced the joys and challenges of parenthood, knowing that the love and bond we shared as a family was worth every moment.

Time seemed to fly by as we watched our children grow and reach significant milestones. Seeing them walk for the first time was a surreal experience, filled with pride and wonder at the wonders of life. It amazed us how quickly they progressed from barely walking toddlers to energetic and curious explorers at 18 months old. Parenthood was a rollercoaster of emotions, filled with both joy and challenges, but we cherished every moment and looked forward to witnessing their growth and development in the years to come.

When my daughters were just toddlers, I eagerly introduced them to the excitement of hiking and skiing. I remember getting special skis and boots for Madison and pulling her around the ski area, her laughter echoing through the snow-covered slopes.

We shared countless moments together, from skiing down the mountain, side by side, to hiking in the woods on my back. As they grew older, our adventures expanded, and I marveled at their resilience and determination.

Madison was only four years old when she hiked her first real mountain, and Jacie, a bit more stubborn, eventually embraced skiing, too. Their growth and achievements filled me with immense pride, but at the same time, I couldn't help but think of the future and the financial responsibilities that would come with it. College expenses seemed like a distant concern, but I couldn't escape the worry lurking in my mind.

As they continued to grow, we shared unforgettable experiences together. We took trips to Florida and Disney World, spent time at the lake, and enjoyed skiing trips, creating cherished memories as a family. I taught them to swim, and their mother, Judy, played an integral role in their nurturing and upbringing.

They are both young adults. Madison is 25, and Jacie is 23. Reflecting on their journey, I am in awe of how quickly time has flown by. It feels like they were little girls just yesterday, and now they have become successful, independent individuals. I miss those earlier days dearly, the laughter, the adventures, and the joy we experienced as a close-knit family.

Us

Chapter 9: In the Sky

My love for flying began when I glided as a teenager and felt the thrill of feeling weightless and seamlessly drifting through the sky.

My mom was the one who introduced me to it after she had first taken lessons. I was around 14 years old at the time, and it was one of the best moments of my life at the time. Later on, skydiving always appealed to me, even as a teenager.

I finally decided to try it with some friends when I was 22. But when the time came, most of them changed their minds, and only a few of us went. Before going on a plane, we first had to learn the dos and don'ts of skydiving in a classroom for about 8 hours. The classroom was in a garage because the place where we were learning was new, and it didn't have everything ready yet. There were things like airplane propellers on the walls and parachute gear hanging from the ceiling.

While we were cooped up in the classroom, learning the safety measures of skydiving, some experienced people started jumping from a plane. We heard voices from the sky and saw parachutes coming down. Although I was only seeing them while still planted to the ground, it made me giddy, thinking that I would soon be gearing up and on one of these planes, anticipating my first-ever jump.

Soon, we finished our classes, and it was my turn to experience skydiving. The plane could hold three people who jumped. The pilot, the jumpmaster, and three jumpers. We were hooked to the plane with a static line. They picked me to go first because I was the heaviest, to keep the plane balanced.

As I sat there, filled with mixed emotions – a blend of nervousness and excitement overpowered me. When we jumped, the static line pulled the parachute out. So, it was a parachute jump, not a free fall. As we ascended, my heart raced within me during the 10-minute journey. The jump master, my guide, ensured my line was secure, and with a sense of anticipation, he swung open the door.

Now, imagine this: I was seated, facing the plane's rear. I extended my feet outside when the door opened to my left, just below the wing. It was a moment of intense disbelief and a feeling of "Whoa, hang on!" They had taught us to put our feet on the step above the landing wheel, and I followed their instructions as best I could. The wind was hurricane-force, and the air was chilled.

I glanced at the jump master, and he signaled, "Go!" I did a quick double-take as if to say, "Wait, me?" Of course, it had to be me since I was the only one at the door, yet fear lingered.

Summoning all of my courage, I took a deep breath and leaped. Eyes shut, I plunged into the unknown and kept my eyes shut until I felt a powerful jolt accompanying the parachute unfurling above me. Looking up, I saw it spread wide and steady.

In that fleeting instant, it was hard to grasp. I had truly accomplished it! My entire body felt alive, and I was buzzing with adrenaline. Locating the airport, I noticed the large bright orange arrow on the field, helping me to navigate. It was a special bright orange, 20-foot-long arrow on a pivot where the ground instructor would point it in the appropriate directions. A radio in my helmet allowed the voice from the ground to guide me, serving as a backup to the arrow's direction. I aimed according to the arrow's guidance.

I remained suspended in the sky for a brief span, just a few minutes. I looked around at the scenery and was allowed to spin my parachute for an extra thrill. I realized that I was flying like a bird under a parachute shaped like a wing. Then, the time arrived to land. Upon landing, I ran like a 50-yard dash, determined not to stumble. And guess what? I didn't fall!

As my feet finally touched the earth, an overwhelming surge of euphoria engulfed me. I couldn't help but think, "Wow, that's easily the most amazing thing I've ever accomplished!" I was so excited and knew I had to do it again. My friends felt the same way when they landed.

So, I began counting down the days till the next week when I would get to do this all over again. It's like my mind was stuck on that incredible experience. The next day, my friend Ron and I decided that we could not wait for that long, and we hopped in the car and drove back to Maine from Massachusetts. We did another jump, and that was when I knew this was it – I was completely hooked. I had found something outside of my drinking and depression, which gave me a better rush without the curse of the hangover afterward. I started thinking about learning to do free fall, which became an all-consuming focus.

After that point, which was in the fall of '86, things started to change. I went up into the sky again the next weekend and did my first free-fall jump. It was much different than the parachute jumps. Learning to fall stable through the sky at 120 MPH is not simple or natural. My brain was overwhelmed with excitement and fear. It was a cold, harsh, loud, frightening environment and WONDERFUL all at the same time. You are trained to arch your body with your belly out to fall like a badminton birdie to stay in the stable stomach-to-earth position. Two jumpmasters are with you for the entire freefall, giving hand signals to adjust your body positions and to pull your ripcord if you don't. I didn't on my first freefall. I had a brainfreeze moment. It was much more intense than expected. My consecutive jumps were perfect after really knowing what to expect.

I found a way to make it work financially by getting paid for packing parachutes, and that payment translated into credits I could use for more jumps. So, by packing parachutes, I could pay for my skydiving adventures. And let me tell you, it became a way of life for me, especially that winter when I first began jumping. My addictive personality had found a way to get the adrenaline rush, and I would not let this go.

When the weather got colder up north, the drop zone where I learned closed for the winter season. Some people head to warmer places like California or Florida for the winter. I went to Florida, California, and Arizona that winter and spring with a group of new friends. It was during that first year that I managed to complete a whopping 400 jumps!

Before long, I took on a new role as a jump master. This meant I was guiding people to jump out of the plane, just like my jump master did for me. I also became a free fall jumpmaster, which meant I was there to help and guide someone through their instructional free fall jumps. I'd make sure they followed the instructions, even though they were scared, and overcome their inhibitions to conquer their fears and truly enjoy the experience of jumping out of planes. I'd teach them how to position their body correctly and pull the cord at the right time.

Then came the next step: I earned my tandem instructor rating. This meant I had to prove my skills on the job. An examiner watched as I took a passenger on a jump. My "guinea pig" passenger was Judy, my girlfriend, now my wife.

Both of us had a real craving for adventure, but the idea of being responsible for our lives during that jump filled me with apprehension and excitement. We traveled to Pennsylvania for this challenge, my first tandem jump.

As we left the plane, things got a bit more nerve-wracking. I had failed to secure Judy tightly enough, so she shifted underneath me when we jumped. We turned into a spinning propeller, causing us to spin around in free fall. I tried to slow it down, but it kept getting faster. I grew increasingly worried, but the examiner who followed us slowed the spin by hitting my legs just as I opened the parachute. This was perfect timing, which avoided the likelihood of major line twists.

Although it had a slight twist, I fixed it, and we landed safely without any injuries. This gave me the confidence boost I needed, and we continued with a few more jumps like that, and eventually, I became a certified tandem instructor.

Skydiving was quickly becoming a big part of my life, something I did on top of my other job, and it was a big responsibility that I now had to manage. This new gig allowed me to get paid for doing my favorite activity, jumping out of planes.

Skydiving was a blast, especially when we added the fun of doing formations. Imagine this: Sometimes, up to 100 people would jump together out of several airplanes in formation, and we'd create these planned, choreographed shapes while falling through the sky. It was like a dance in the air that we all accomplished together. We even set some new records in New England for our formations – that was quite a thrill.

Freefall formation record, the mid-1990s

Beyond the regular jumps, I found a lot of enjoyment in what they call "demo jumps." These are jumps where you perform at events like fairs or air shows. People would hire us to add an extra level of excitement to their events. Believe it or not, there was even a time when I got paid to jump into a nudist park, not once, but twice, along with some other jumpers. Yes, I jumped nude! So you see, there's a ton of fun and adventure in skydiving beyond just the regular practice or being an instructor.

Around the same time as tandem jumping, I also learned how to fly airplanes. It was a busy, thrilling time!

During the tandem jump with friends in 1990

After I decided to learn how to fly planes, it didn't take too long, as my love for flying helped me pursue my dreams relentlessly. I got my pilot's license in under a year and would fly whenever possible, even on short trips, to gain experience. After getting my license, I continuously learned.

The first big moment was flying alone. I had to take off and land all by myself. I remember the instructor leaving the plane on the ground, and there I was, flying solo, doing touch-and-go landings. It's like landing and then taking off again over and over. It was an exhilarating experience, knowing I was the only thing controlling this big machine, and even the simplest mistake could send it crashing down.

Next came the cross-country flights, where I flew about 100 miles to one airport, then 200 miles to another, and back where I began, covering around 500 miles total. I had to find someone to sign my logbook at each airport to prove my journey. Being someone who loved flying, I will forever remember that experience—plotting a course, focusing on the route while watching out for other aircraft through the skies, and fulfilling lifelong dreams. I would be on top of the world during those flights, feeling a high that no substance can make you feel.

Flying at night was a whole new experience. It was dark, and you rely on instruments and ground lights, which can be tricky. I once flew over the ocean at night. It felt difficult to tell up from down in the blackness. I thought it was cool to control the runway lights from the plane using the microphone. I could adjust them, make them brighter, dimmer, or even blink.

I often brought Judy and other friends along on these flights to different destinations. Every distance and problem felt minuscule when you had access to a plane. We'd fly all day sometimes, enjoying the serene skies and landscapes, and land in random places throughout New England for breakfast or lunch. It was a fun way to explore together.

That period marked the beginning of a significant chapter in my life – a time filled with flying and skydiving adventures that spanned roughly 15 to 20 years. From that first jump to the very last, it was a period that shaped me in so many ways. However, flying airplanes wasn't something I did too often. It was exciting, no doubt, but renting a plane quickly added up and was a financial decision I couldn't repeatedly make while supporting a family.

Taking off and soaring through the skies, just exploring without a set plan, came with a hefty price tag each time. But the flying I did while piloting jump aircraft was a different story. It was gaining free flying time, a delightful bonus. Most of my hours in the air were spent maneuvering a Cessna 182, carrying jumpers to the skies.

As much as I loved it, skydiving and flying the jumps could be demanding. It wasn't just about the thrill; it involved a lot of responsibility. You have someone's safety in your hands when they're attached to you during a jump and as a pilot in command of an aircraft. Gradually, this stress accumulated, and I found myself stepping back. I shifted my focus towards nurturing my family and growing my business.

Over time, I started to phase out both skydiving and flying. After spending nearly 20 years in the sport, I took a break, with my last jump and flying experiences ending around the same time. My last flight was with my 3-year-old daughter, Madison, in the back seat. My love for the skies never ended, and I am still just as passionate as ever, but I recognized that my favorite hobby had started to feel like a chore to me, and I needed to focus on my business and family to move on and explore other horizons.

Decades later, I still haven't lost my desire to fly. In fact, I recently re-started my flying lessons. I am now a solo glider pilot, very close to achieving my license. Ever since an unforgettable glider flight over Mt. Washington, NH, in the mid-1990s, where I soared up to 20,000 feet with the strong winds blowing the glider high above the summit into a lenticular cloud, I have yearned to pursue the sport...and now a lifetime dream is coming true!

Chapter 10: Struggle with Addiction and Mental Health

My dependency on alcohol as a coping mechanism started when the bullying began in high school. I would turn to alcohol to take the edge off of the depression and anxiety. After realizing my problems, I recognized my need to stay busy to keep myself distracted, so I started exploring other activities to stay busy and sober. It was when I got into skydiving and scuba diving to distract my adrenaline-seeking mind.

Although skydiving didn't stop me from drinking, it did bring the biggest blessing in my life: my beautiful wife and our relationship, which resulted in our beautiful family.

My problem controlling my alcohol consumption continued into my adult life. Still, it worsened after my battle with depression and anxiety started, pushing me into a deeper hole of despair, which I would try to fix by forgetting my problems and drinking the night away.

I met different people from all walks of life when I started skydiving. Some professionals, such as doctors, accountants, dentists, and airline pilots, some like me, and some in between. We all had the same thing in common. We loved to skydive, chase adrenaline, and socialize over some alcohol at the end of the day. Over time, I developed a liking for pot. It mixed nicely with alcohol, too. I liked it even more during outdoor physical activities like hiking and skiing. It made me feel focused. I was always careful with all substances when it came to flying and skydiving, except for one time.

Eventually, some harder drugs came into the picture, including cocaine, crystal meth, ecstasy, and mushrooms. It was on the bad weather days, especially when the temptations turned into instant gratification for me.

I liked cocaine the most for a while until it made me paranoid and started to get out of control. Mushrooms made me sick. Crystal meth had the most side effects for me. It burned my nostrils when I snorted it and kept me awake for days after I tried it, and that experience was enough to keep me away from it. I did a demo jump in Texas while on meth, which was stupid and the last time I tried it. Fortunately, it was mostly just one summer that I indulged with substances. I could feel how cocaine (especially) could have consumed me.

As my depression and anxiety grew, my marriage bore the heavy toll of my emotional turmoil. Regrettably, it felt like a gradual descent into darkness, and I was pulling my innocent family down into the depths of my despair.

There came a pivotal point when each morning became a battlefield just to get out of bed. I'd half-heartedly make phone calls and check emails, wrapped in the comfort of my blankets. Occasionally, I'd managed to respond to job offers, all while wrapped in the isolating embrace of my bed.

In a peculiar twist of fate, this unorthodox approach seemed effective, if only temporarily. However, my wife's worry intensified as she witnessed my retreat from the world. While I worked less, she shouldered the extra responsibilities to make up for our dwindling income.

This cycle began innocently. I'd have job prospects lined up, but an overwhelming dread would paralyze me on the appointed day. It wasn't rooted in a night of drinking but rather in the deteriorating state of my mind and body. So, I'd make secretive calls or send messages to reschedule, citing various reasons.

My decline and weight gain in 2019

Surprisingly, clients often understood, but I kept this hidden truth from my wife. When she inquired about my work for the day, I feigned indifference, stating that they had rescheduled the job. In reality, I was rearranging the rubble of my life behind her back, trapped in a spiral of self-destruction.

At times, I was embarking on work assignments, often in the bustling state of New York or even farther afield. These opportunities held an undeniable allure, as they allowed me to venture into uncharted territories, a glimmer of hope and motivation amidst the prevailing storm of my struggles.

However, with the passage of each day during these excursions, an unsettling pattern began to unfold. Typically, when I had a job in New York, I would be absent from the familiar comforts of home for three to four days. As night descended and my work obligations concluded, I would consistently seek refuge in a hotel room.

In this solitude, my solace was a six-pack of beer and a selection of wines and pot. Serving as my companions for the night. It was as though these alcoholic indulgences were my sole means of achieving a semblance of closure, a coping mechanism to help me confront the day's formidable challenges.

Concurrently, another development was taking shape, distressingly evident through a noticeable increase in my body weight. This physical transformation served as a tangible reflection of the inner turmoil and unhealthy coping strategies that had begun to permeate and define my existence.

As the grip of anxiety and depression tightened its hold on me, my once hearty appetite dwindled to near nothingness. It was an odd paradox because while I rarely consumed fulfilling meals, my absurd habits of excessive drinking wreaked havoc on my physique. I barely ate, but the alcohol became an unwelcome friend that stealthily added to my weight without the slightest assistance from exercise. The truth was, I had lost all motivation to move, to do anything at all, my depression in full control of my body. I felt like my body had a mind of its own, and I was trapped in this shell, which I didn't recognize, watching helplessly from the sidelines as my poor decisions caught up to me. Eventually, I reached a grim point where I had to muster the strength to force myself into work. Dread clung to me like a relentless shadow throughout the day. It was so suffocating that I'd escape to my van, retching violently despite my empty stomach.

I'd dry heave in hiding, unwilling to let anyone witness my anguish. Returning to work, the days felt endless, filled with mistakes and a noticeable decline in the quality of my work. Callbacks from customers became more frequent, and the repairs I had to undertake were never quite up to par. Even something as simple as replacing window film felt like an impossible task.

Texting became my lifeline, a more comfortable form of communication over the years. I initially dismissed it as a trivial habit, but it soon became an obsession, perhaps even another disorder to add to my growing list.

Yet, my job prospects dwindled steadily, further exacerbating my anxiety about work. This, in turn, pushed me deeper into the clutches of alcohol, perpetuating a toxic cycle from which escape seemed impossible.

I distinctly recall how my wife had to shoulder an ever-increasing workload to the extent that she eventually transitioned into a full-time role as an accountant. Finances grew increasingly tight, and my frequent visits to the doctor for my depression only exacerbated our financial strain.

The gentle exchanges through text messages morphed into emotional shouting matches typed out on our screens. The escalation didn't stop there; soon, the heated words found their voice in verbal confrontations. My actions had begun to cast a dark shadow over our marriage, and I was at a loss on how to mend it. It felt like I was sinking beneath the weight of my problems, with no capacity left to accommodate any additional concerns on my already overflowing plate. The sense of drowning in my troubles was suffocating, leaving me adrift in a sea of despair, unable to find a lifeline to pull us back together.

I reached a point where I no longer contributed to our household income. I'd venture out, feigning being busy in a field where work couldn't be done on a whim. Sure, you can plant seeds for future opportunities, a tactic I had used in the past, but when there's no work to be found, there's simply no work.

Day after day, I struggled to fill my time, attempting to mask the truth that I was essentially going out to pretend to work. I would often make one stop and then idly sit in parking lots, wrestling with the overwhelming uncertainty of my situation. And then, a text from my wife would jolt me back to reality: "Have you found any work?" My responses evolved from "I might have something in the works for next week, maybe," to increasingly vague assurances.

Over time, my escalating anxiety provided a twisted justification for picking up a few beers. It dulled the edge of my worries, if only temporarily. I started to hide beers in different places around the house and secretly used to drink them. I'd sit in my van, grappling with the broken promise I made to myself never to drink and drive again. Yet, I found myself doing just that, sinking deeper into a cycle tearing our marriage apart.

At this point, I sought more help from my psychologist and psychiatrist, desperately seeking guidance. I'd lay out all my problems, and their advice was straightforward: "You should try to find a regular job, maybe at Walmart or Home Depot, just to reintroduce a sense of normalcy into your life." But the prospect of working for someone else, of being judged by others, sent my anxious mind into a tailspin. It felt like an insurmountable hurdle, yet another obstacle in a life already overrun by obstacles.

The very idea of working under someone else's authority seemed like an insurmountable hurdle. I had never experienced taking orders from anyone other than myself throughout the entirety of my life. Even managing my own business had evolved into an uphill struggle. How could I possibly entertain the notion of working for another, especially given the weight of my ongoing challenges?

Nevertheless, the truth remained undeniably evident. It was the logical course of action I should have been capable of pursuing. Yet, I found myself immobilized by this concept. Alongside this existential crisis, the menacing specter of healthcare expenses loomed. Each visit to the doctor drained my financial resources further, as I had not yet reached the deductible.

I had to issue a check for $106 every occasion, an amount I did not possess. I borrowed money from my business to cover this expense, perpetuating an illogical financial cycle that spiraled out of control. I understood that I was in a desperate situation, but I still hadn't caught up to the extent of the damage alcohol had on my life.

Then, there was no more money. I couldn't pay my bills. My credit cards and business line of credit were maxed out, and the debt collectors started calling and demanding payment. My once top-notch credit history became bottom-of-the-barrel.

Alcoholism and depression had firmly ensnared my life, and I remained baffled about how to free myself from their grip. My counselors provided advice, well-intentioned but ultimately unhelpful in the context of my unique circumstances. Then, a pivotal moment arrived when my wife took it upon herself to research a rehabilitation facility, Hampstead Hospital, designed to assist those struggling with substance abuse and mental health challenges. I was vehemently against being admitted to an institution, not accepting that my situation couldn't be fixed through some therapy and required a thorough intervention.

Not shortly after that, a project I had undertaken in Maine deteriorated despite my two prior attempts to salvage it, ultimately resulting in a dispute with the contractor. They demanded my return and even sent a threatening legal notice, which I concealed from my wife. It felt like this would be the last straw for a disastrous climax of our marriage, and I was consumed with guilt and despair.

Confronted by the weight of my failures and an impending sense of hopelessness, I was riddled with anxiety and decided to take a leap of faith and check into the hospital ER my counselor had recommended, despite not knowing what awaited me there. It was a desperate and uncertain step into uncharted territory, but it appeared to be the sole remaining option on a growing increasingly dangerous path.

My first visit to the hospital was a daunting experience. I arrived at the Emergency Room, my heart pounding with anxiety. My counselor had emphasized the importance of keeping her informed, so she instructed me to call her and share what transpired during my visit. I nervously complied, determined to stay connected with her guidance. As I entered the hospital, I felt an overwhelming sense of being put on the spot.

The medical staff wasted no time; they could see I needed help. It was clear that they couldn't simply release me without a plan. They gave me choices: a 30-day program, detox, or an evaluation to determine if detox was necessary, followed by extended treatment. Alternatively, I could continue my ongoing treatment with my counselor. I was torn between my desire to avoid the unknown and my fear of entering a facility.

In the end, I chose to stick with my counselor's guidance. The prospect of going elsewhere was just too intimidating. However, over the following two months, my condition deteriorated significantly. Sleep had become a distant memory, with weeks passing by without rest. I roamed the basement restlessly, seeking solace in an occasional beer, although its relief was painfully fleeting, lasting mere minutes or not at all.

In desperation, I decided to seek help at Hampstead Hospital. As I sat there, a nurse handed me a questionnaire, urging me to answer honestly. If I was there for treatment, honesty was paramount.

The questions delved into the darkest corners of my mind, including whether I had ever contemplated taking my own life. I admitted to having suicidal thoughts, although not in the sense of wanting to end my life immediately. Instead, I yearned for a peaceful, eternal slumber free from the gruesome imagery of self-inflicted harm.

As I contemplated my responses, I anxiously awaited their evaluation. When they returned, they asked for the keys to my van. I questioned their intent, and they explained it was to move my vehicle. Initially, I resisted, but it became evident that they didn't want me to leave and were legally obligated to prevent my departure. The realization struck me like a sledgehammer, and I was overcome with mortification and horror. I was confined, not in jail, but in a psych ward, uncertain how long I would remain within its walls.

The ward was filled with a diverse mix of young and old individuals, but I found myself standing out as one of the older occupants. As I settled into my bed, I relished having the room to myself, even briefly. However, the tranquility was consistently interrupted.

The hospital staff, be it nurses or attendants, diligently patrolled the corridors, and it seemed like they checked on me every 10 minutes throughout the night. Their routine consisted of opening my door to ensure I was alright. They had given me medication to aid my sleep, but the frequent door openings and the blinding flashlight beams that accompanied them rendered rest nearly impossible. It was an absurd situation, and I understood the necessity for their vigilance, yet it felt torturous.

Confined within the walls of this facility, I couldn't help but wonder about the duration of my stay. Thoughts raced through my mind: Was I now a ward of the state? Would I be confined in a place like this forever? In my distorted mental state, fueled by depression and many other factors, I genuinely believed that I might never leave. Despite my wife's reassurances that it would likely be just another week or two, I was convinced that I was facing a lifetime of imprisonment.

My thoughts were trapped in a web of irrationality, a manifestation of my deteriorating mental health. I couldn't think logically about certain aspects of my situation. It was painfully evident, and I remained trapped within my distorted reality. However, as it turned out, I eventually left that place eight long days later. Yet, this was not a straightforward process.

The medical team regulated my medications during my stay and conducted ongoing evaluations. They meticulously observed my progress, waiting for the moment they deemed me ready to be released back into the world. When that moment finally arrived, they provided recommendations for my next steps, suggesting outpatient care and meetings to help me on the path to recovery, a glimmer of hope amid the tumultuous storm of my life.

Although the hospital stay felt like a nuisance then, I understood its importance. This is why the discharge came suddenly as if they had anticipated a miraculous recovery within a week. Their words were brief, stating, "It's time to leave," while providing recommendations for the path ahead, including outpatient care and daily therapy sessions. Instantly, I was thrust back into the world, confronted with the formidable challenge of independently continuing my rehabilitation journey.

The recommended outpatient facility was a 45-minute drive away, and I approached it skeptically. I examined their treatment approach, which included conventional methods like art therapy involving crayons and drawing. My initial response was one of disbelief. Internally, I pondered, "Are they serious? Can crayons and drawing truly aid my recovery? It seems suitable for a preschooler, not a person like me." I carried a resistant attitude, finding the concept utterly preposterous.

The treatment program also encompassed group meetings, which I found more manageable than the art therapy sessions. Nevertheless, I detested the clinical environment and the sensation of being a patient in that setting. After only a week there, my wife, in collaboration with my best friend, John, and his wife, Amanda, organized for me to stay with them for a period. Understandably, my wife didn't want our children to witness my fragile state and my struggles with suicidal thoughts. Though it wasn't my preference, I at least had the company of my best friend and his family.

I ended up living with them for over a year and a half. During this period, my sleep patterns remained erratic. There were phases when I couldn't sleep for seven or even nine consecutive days. Approximately two months into my stay with John and Amanda, I found myself seated in my van in a parking lot, my business signs adorning the vehicle. To my right, I spotted my wife's car pulling up, an entirely coincidental encounter far from home.

Intrigued, she inquired, "What are you doing here?" Our brief conversation swiftly escalated into a heated argument. Though the precise words elude my memory, I uttered something deeply unsettled her. Whatever I said instilled fear, prompting her to call the police shortly after departing. At that moment, I hadn't consumed any alcohol, as there was no trace of it in my system. Nonetheless, within ten minutes, a police car with flashing blue lights arrived, and an officer began posing questions, further complicating the turbulence of my already chaotic life.

In a situation fraught with discomfort and unease, I desperately attempted to persuade the police of my well-being despite the undeniable truth that I was far from fine. I donned a façade, weaving a web of pretense to mask my inner turmoil. Their revelation that my wife had voiced concern, thereby divulging my whereabouts, left me grateful and yearning for a swift exit. However, they remained unyielding, unwilling to grant me freedom.

In a desperate bid to preserve my dignity, I implored them to turn off the pulsating blue lights on their patrol vehicle, acutely aware of the growing audience of curious onlookers who had taken notice. The noticeable presence of my company van, with visible business signage, only added to my embarrassment. Their determination to detain me stemmed from their obligation to clarify my motivation. Consequently, they summoned an ambulance from a nearby medical facility, humorously dubbed "Holy Shit" (Holy Family) Hospital in jest.

Upon arriving at the bustling emergency room, many people awaited me. The request for a urine test proved a formidable challenge as I struggled to comply. Time seemed to stretch endlessly as I suffered in that seat, yearning for support. My wife's return offered much-needed solace. Yet, as the night unfolded, I was trapped by an unprecedented, harrowing psychotic episode. What had initially been a minor concern about potential liver issues had now metamorphosed into irrational anxieties, including fear of unwittingly spreading a contagious disease like malaria throughout the hospital. In response to my apprehensions, I was relegated to a solitary room, an anomaly in a facility accustomed to housing patients together. The solitude, while appreciated, couldn't shield me from the hushed conversations among the nurses outside. My paranoia relentlessly whispered that they were discussing me, addressing me as their 'friend.'

Later, as the night pressed on, my bladder's demands became impossible to ignore. Yet, terror held me captive within my room. Ultimately, I succumbed to the overwhelming fear and urinated in a forsaken corner. When the staff discovered the unsavory evidence on camera, they rushed in, demanding an explanation for my silence, leaving me mired in an abyss of shame.

As the night crept forward, the hospital's alarms reverberated ominously through the corridors, magnifying my delusions. In my mind, those alarms heralded the tragic demise of another soul, all because of my imagined contamination. A murky, surreal morning came with the dawn, and I remained convinced that my mere presence had precipitated multiple fatalities. I even overheard the nurses conversing about who would escort "our friend" upstairs, steadfast in my belief that they were referring to me.

Then came a bizarre moment when they placed me in a wheelchair, flanked by two men who navigated me through the labyrinthine hospital. The journey felt endless and irrational terror gripped me as I entertained absurd ideas that they might use a baseball bat against me. It was as if my life had been entangled in a bewildering, orchestrated drama unfolding before my eyes.

Even after this bewildering episode, the memories continued to haunt me. I later discovered that my family and friends were well aware of my predicament. The culmination of ceaseless sleeplessness, mental deterioration, and irrational dread of hospital contamination led to a protracted stay of two and a half weeks in a psychiatric facility. There, I shared quarters with individuals from diverse backgrounds, including those grappling with intellectual disabilities and addiction issues. The depth to which I had plummeted was inconceivable, and the experience proved immensely humbling.

During my stay, my dietary needs necessitated different meals than those offered to the other residents, albeit far from gourmet cuisine. Nevertheless, I accepted it as an integral aspect of my healing process. I endured, and when the time came,

I emerged from the facility, irrevocably altered by the haunting experiences of those tumultuous weeks. During my stay at the psychiatric facility, I received visits from a supportive group, including close friends John and Amanda, as well as my wife and various friends and family members. They provided essential comfort and encouragement during a turbulent period in my life. However, as my discharge date neared, I once again faced the challenges ahead without the specific support I believed was crucial.

I had resisted engaging in therapeutic methods involving crayons and art therapy, struggling to accept the idea of returning to a psychiatric ward. Despite my sincere efforts to make progress, the assistance seemed to fall short of achieving the desired results, and my personal struggles persisted.

Over that year and a half, my life took unexpected and bewildering turns. I had a strange accident, fracturing my ankle after tripping over a flowerpot at John and Amanda's place. My eating habits remained erratic, and I grappled with a drinking problem, often escaping to parking lots under the pretense of job hunting to avoid constant company. These episodes were marked by overwhelming unease, and I felt myself descending into my old behavior due to my depression.

I got up one winter morning and saw that my van was gone. I thought it was stolen at first, but the police told me that my bank repossessed it. It felt like another seemingly endless strike against me. Thanks to my loving mother, I was able to get it back.

There were nights when I contemplated living out of my van, even during the bitter winter months. I resorted to keeping the engine running, often running out of gas to stay warm. To my surprise, John consistently tracked me down, discreetly installing a tracking app to my phone out of genuine concern for my safety.

John's remarkable sense of humor and ability to inject laughter into any situation became a lifeline during these trying times. His wife, Amanda, stood as an unwavering pillar of support. Despite spending a year and a half under their care, I felt unprepared to move forward.

I eventually secured a job in the window film industry, working for a company specializing in car window tinting and paint protection. While expanding into window film for buildings sounded promising, the work proved monotonous and dull. My boss, a 22-year-old with limited knowledge of window film, left me feeling out of place and often humiliated. Despite my inner turmoil, I had to maintain a facade of normalcy. My ordeal took a painful turn when, after approximately six weeks, a freak accident left me with another broken ankle and excruciating pain.

During one restless night, as was my habit, I attempted to get a drink from my dark apartment, only to encounter further misfortune when the faucet broke, spraying water everywhere. In agony and with a broken ankle, I managed to halt the water flow, but I was left lying in the darkness, grappling with insurmountable challenges and a large sense of hopelessness.

This period also marked the escalation of my late-night texts, which became increasingly erratic and, at times, hostile. On her journey of healing, my wife distanced herself from me, intensifying my feelings of isolation and despair. I became convinced that the solution to my problems lay solely within myself and that I was the only one capable of helping me. Yet, I wrestled with overwhelming mental and physical obstacles, yearning for a solution that remained frustratingly elusive.

I often composed texts, pouring out my emotions into messages I never intended to send. The late hours seemed endless as insomnia gripped me, and I felt the relentless urge to do something, anything.

The texting habit morphed into a significant issue. The morning after the pivotal accident that fractured my ankle, John brought me to the hospital, limping with pain. The doctor's verdict was unequivocal – a broken ankle. They fitted me with a walking cast and conducted a walking test. Meanwhile, the job I had been struggling with made a stark decision. They terminated my employment because I hadn't immediately informed them of my injury. Concern had swiftly turned to dismissal.

Oddly, I felt a sense of relief mingled with disappointment because I despised that job but knew how important it was for the financial stability of my household. My healing journey posed its challenges. A precarious staircase connected my apartment on the third floor. With slippery steps outside and cramped quarters indoors, I was forced to sit and scoot down on my rear to navigate them. The ordeal was exacerbated by the fact that I couldn't walk properly.

Every venture outdoors became a chore, prompting me to stock up on beer to minimize the need for frequent trips up and down the stairs. However, five weeks into the healing process, I noticed a troubling escalation of pain in my leg. Initially dismissing it as a normal part of the healing process, I eventually turned to Google for answers.

The search results were far from reassuring, pointing to the possibility of deep vein thrombosis (DVT) or blood clots. Reluctantly, I headed to the emergency room. They conducted an ultrasound there, revealing a massive clot that extended from my ankle to my groin.

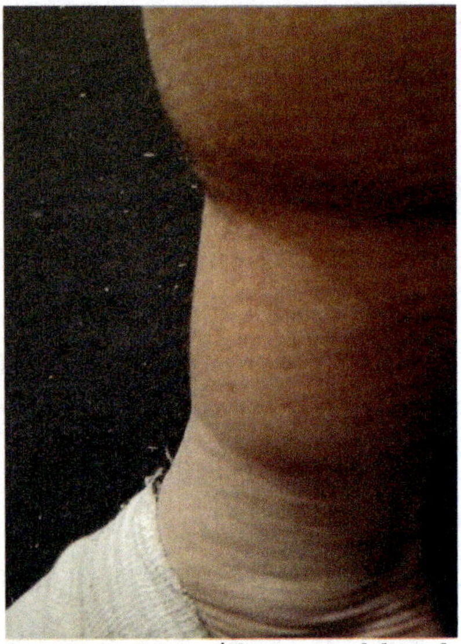

My damaged leg (due to a blood clot)

It was a frightening diagnosis, and further examinations revealed that the clot had resulted in a pulmonary embolism affecting my lungs.

Remarkably, I had felt no symptoms from the embolism, no coughing or distress. Yet, the reality struck me – this condition could have been fatal. A part of me even wished it had been, considering the overwhelming challenges I faced. For two harrowing weeks, I found myself in the intensive care unit, undergoing surgeries and confronting the fragility of life.

In the depths of despair, I had embarked on a tumultuous journey through the labyrinth of my struggles. Each twist and turn led me to unforeseen challenges, from the confines of a psychiatric facility to a shattered ankle and the discovery of life-threatening blood clots.

As I emerged from this chapter of my life, battered but not beaten, I carried with me the profound understanding that the path to recovery was fraught with hardships. It was a journey that I couldn't undertake alone, and it was a journey that had only just begun.

Chapter 11: Journey to Sobriety

I had been faithfully attending sessions with my psychologist, seeking solace in her guidance, when one day, I made the decision to skip an appointment, considering it a minor deviation in the grand scheme of things. Little did I anticipate that this choice would soon land me in a whirlpool of concern.

Out of the blue, my psychologist phoned me, her voice heavy with concern, urging me to rush to the hospital. My heart pounded, anxiety taking hold as she revealed the shocking news - she had contacted the police due to worries about my safety when I missed our session. At that moment, I truly grasped the seriousness of the situation.

Overwhelmed by fear and confusion, I left my home before the authorities arrived. She pleaded with me to go to the emergency room, leaving me torn between fear and hesitation. The memories of previous stays in the psychiatric ward haunted me, and I expressed my reluctance to return.

Me at my lowest point in 2020

She reassured me, building trust with her gentle yet resolute demeanor. She promised that this time would be different, assuring me that the hospital staff had no intention of admitting me to the psychiatric ward. My mind swirled with emotions - fear, trust, and a glimmer of hope that this unexpected twist might signal a turning point in my path to recovery.

Me during my first year of recovery, 2021

Upon reaching the hospital, a mix of anticipation and anxiety overwhelmed me. My first move was to inform my psychologist of my presence. What happened next left me in disbelief. They promptly returned me to the very place I had hoped to avoid, extending my stay for another agonizing ten days. It felt like a profound breach of trust, as I had explicitly shared my traumatic experience in the psych ward with my therapist and explained that my only reason for agreeing to go was her assurance about not being readmitted.

I found myself back there without my consent, holding onto the hope that, this time, things would be different. During this prolonged period, the routine remained largely unchanged - the psych ward housed a new group of individuals, each grappling with their unique struggles. My primary concern was a potentially dangerous blood clot, which the medical team addressed with blood thinners. As I awaited discharge, they unexpectedly tasked me with the unsettling responsibility of administering my own injections.

When I had been admitted, they initiated a procedure common in such cycles - the meticulous inventorying of personal belongings. They meticulously itemized everything, from money to credit cards to my phone, wallet, and keys. I went through the process, signing off on each item.

However, after ten long and emotionally draining days, when the moment came for my departure, a chilling revelation struck me like a bolt of lightning - my possessions were no longer secure in the hospital's vault and had gone missing. Panic and frustration surged through me as I realized that everything I held dear had vanished, although the wallet was empty and the credit cards were no longer active. They couldn't simply release me into the world without my belongings, especially my car keys, which left me stranded and forced to overstay in a place where I had been kept against my will for the last ten days. The mere recollection of that nightmarish experience causes my blood pressure to rise, underscoring the profound impact it had on me.

As I emerged from the hospital, a pivotal day marked the start of my next chapter. I relocated to Boston, where I took up residence with my friend Ron. Our shared house became my sanctuary for the next half-year. However, life within those walls unfolded like a recurring story, echoing the past. It felt like no matter how hard I tried, my previous life would always catch up with me.

During my stay there, it was a familiar scene - a revolving door of individuals, most of whom had a troubling affinity for drugs. Ron, a good-hearted soul himself, had friends who occasionally paid visits, and regrettably, most of them were stuck in addiction. This environment, rife with temptation and instability, was far from ideal for my journey to recovery.

This was also when my wife pushed for our divorce, and we made it official with the help of a mediator. This was crushing for me, and I tried to avoid it. I didn't want a divorce, but at the same time, I couldn't blame her for being done with me. I was also done with me. It wasn't fair for her to be continuously ensnared in my never-ending self-inflicted misery and chaos. I will always consider this my greatest loss.

My marriage was once my greatest gain and pride. I will always wish Judy the best. She is an amazing, strong person and a loving mother.

Meanwhile, my sister, desperately trying to reach me, tried to contact my phone, but I had no phone, thanks to the unfortunate incident at the hospital. Remember, they had custom keys made for my van and a meager ten dollars for gas, utterly neglecting their responsibility for the loss of my possessions, which were painstakingly cataloged during my admission.

In the midst of this turmoil, my sister Jen grew increasingly worried, and not knowing what else to do, she resorted to calling the police on me to conduct a wellness check. I had texted her from my iPad the night before, saying something that worried her. It was a fateful morning when I was sprawled on the couch, the knock on the door and unfamiliar voices jolting me from my daydream. Two officers stood before me, addressing me as Mr. Harlow. I affirmed my identity, puzzled by their presence.

Their visit, it turned out, was a wellness check, and their concern was palpable. They had summoned an ambulance, intent on ferrying me back to the hospital. I strongly resisted, insisting that I hadn't done anything wrong. Their eyes fell upon the beer bottles on the counter, probing, "Are those your beer bottles?" I retorted, "People here drink beer, but why is that your concern?" The situation was uncomfortable, an intrusion into my life.

Although I understood that they were merely executing their duty, I didn't want to go with them and risk being readmitted to the psych hospital. I vehemently declined the ambulance, signing a waiver that essentially stated my refusal of the offered assistance.

I welcomed this opportunity to break free from their intervention, as the thought of reliving the cycle of the psychiatric ward was unbearable. At that point in my life, I believed such interventions were counterproductive for me, yearning for the liberty to address my issues without the constraints of a psychiatric ward.

After rejecting the police during the wellness check incident, I continued living with my friend Ron. Little did I anticipate another twist in the narrative of my life was on the horizon.

You see, Ron had undertaken the responsibility of caring for his father in the house we shared. The house actually belonged to Ron's brother. Following his father's death, Ron got some money from his father's inheritance and decided to vacate his brother's house. Half a year had passed since that loss, and Ron had started to focus on his own dreams and aspirations again. He yearned for a place to call his own and utilized a portion of his inheritance to acquire a mobile home.

Ron's decision to relocate marked a pivotal moment in our lives. He understood the gravity of my situation and the depth of my struggles and was genuinely concerned for my well-being. Although he would have preferred me to remain with him, he recognized that my primary problem was the need for professional assistance for recovery. Consequently, I couldn't join him as initially intended.

During this period, I reconnected with an old acquaintance on Facebook, Gregg, who I knew from working at one of the car dealerships where I had formerly been involved in tinting and applying stripes to vehicles. When I reached out to him, he extended a lifeline, taking into account the circumstances.

Amidst my recent divorce proceedings and the tumultuous state of my life, he was also grappling with the challenges of his own divorce. He generously offered me temporary accommodation, which I accepted with reluctance despite profound discomfort and embarrassment. At that point, I weighed 315 pounds and was very insecure, dealing with body image issues and trying to get my life back on track.

My three-month stay with him was marked by my efforts to maintain a low profile. Overwhelming self-consciousness compelled me to avoid his presence frequently. Whenever he left the premises, I would escape into my van, aimlessly driving around.

Not long after, my miserable circumstances led me to a corner where I found myself reverting to old habits, seeking solace in alcohol once more as a desperate coping mechanism for the turbulent journey I was navigating.

In an eternal struggle, I found myself trapped within an unyielding and maddening rut, an affliction that had relentlessly gnawed at me. This suffering persisted until a defining moment arose.

It was a night of pouring rain, as though nature itself wept in anticipation of the judgment that loomed over me. I sat alone in my dimly illuminated car, a dangerous mix of vodka and beer coursing through my veins, filling me with a reckless blend of despair and numbness. The road ahead, obscured by the eerie glow of my headlights, seemed to blur in front of my eyes, much like the intricate path my life had taken.

As fate would have it, my self-destructive choices led me to drive my car down into a ditch, a symbol of the emotional abyss that had engulfed me. The car shuddered upon impact with a lamppost, seemingly highlighting the wreckage that my life had become.

I remained trapped, both within my vehicle and within the shadows of my soul, with raindrops tracing forlorn patterns on the windshield.

Terror gripped me as the red and blue lights, flashing in the night, transformed it into a foreboding canvas. The sirens grew louder, drawing nearer with every heartbeat, serving as a relentless reminder that my actions had finally caught up with me once again. The police were on their way, and I was left with nothing but the oppressive weight of my transgressions.

Then, the breathalyzer test issued a damning verdict: not only had I exceeded the legal limit, but I had done so twofold. Shame and humiliation flooded my senses, submerging me in a sea of self-hatred. It felt as if I had descended to the darkest depths of my being, where the universe itself seemed to cry out, demanding answers to an endless question: "What more could you possibly do wrong?"

An overwhelming yearning for escape surged within me, a longing for release from the never-ending disappointments that had become my life. The void whispered a chilling promise of relief, beckoning me toward the precipice of despair. I yearned for an end to the torment, a desire that resonated deep within me, wanting to escape the judgmental stares of others and escape to a place where my past would stop following me and I would be free of the consequences of my actions. This was just the beginning, a pivotal moment in my turbulent journey. Around three weeks later, I talked with my younger sister Jen, who reached out to me to help me come up with an action plan to turn my life around. I felt like, for the first time in a while, someone had actually cared to ask for my input instead of chucking me into another psych ward.

Together, we devised a plan, a glimmer of hope amidst my despair, for me to pursue treatment at a hospital once more. However, a persistent fear gnawed at me: the fear of returning to the stifling confines of a psychiatric ward.

I was determined not to follow the same worn path that had led me to familiar and haunting scenes. Surrounded by my despair, I found a beacon of hope in McLean's Hospital in Boston. Its reputation in psychiatric care was truly outstanding, renowned, and esteemed for its expertise in managing such sensitive matters. Instead of revisiting my previous hospitalization at Holy Family Hospital, I was briefly admitted to Mass General, where my blood pressure had dangerously spiked to 220 over 200. They administered stabilizing medication and arranged an ambulance to transport me to McLean's.

This marked my fifth encounter with a psychiatric ward, but this time, it felt distinct. I clung to the plan, a lifeline in my life filled with despair, praying that if

I had to be within the walls of a mental health facility, it would be this one. My wish materialized as I entered McLean's Hospital for a week that simultaneously felt everlasting and fleeting.

In many respects, my time at McLean felt like a déjà vu experience. The daily routine, the faces surrounding me, the quest for normalcy in a place designed for the troubled – it all felt eerily familiar. A psychiatric ward, regardless of its reputation or location, is still a psychiatric ward. It was a world inhabited by individuals grappling with their inner demons, a place where the intricacies of the human psyche manifested in countless ways.

Amidst the chaos, the atmosphere crackled with tension, and I found myself thrust into the role of an unexpected peacemaker. It was a turbulent scene, where tempers flared like wildfire, and I stood at the epicenter, bridging the divide.

There were times when I had to break up fights between people. One such incident was when I was forced to intervene between two fighting women. One, driven by anger, leaped across a table, her clenched fists raining blows upon the other woman's head. My heart pounded like a drum, and disbelief washed over me in waves. "Oh, my God," I whispered to myself, in utter disbelief at the lack of humanity I saw in those women's eyes. That day, I understood how mental illnesses strip people of their identity, leaving behind a shell of what once must have been an incredible person. It was a moment that etched itself into my memory, a vivid reminder of the raw human emotions that swirled in the crucible of despair.

As I was struggling through my journey towards sobriety, a lifeline emerged from the digital realm, where a perceptive Facebook friend, someone from my high school days, recognized the turmoil within me through my cryptic online posts. In a private message, she offered me advice that altered the course of my rehabilitation journey. "Look into dual diagnosis treatment," her words echoed in my mind like a beacon of hope.

Fast forward to the end of my stay at McLean's Hospital, where a list of potential paths forward was placed before me. Among the options, the term "dual diagnosis" appeared in parentheses several times. It was a crossroads, a profound leap of faith, for I had lost everything. My pockets were empty, and I had entered the hospital with no more than a pair of underwear, shorts, and a simple T-shirt. I was penniless, stripped of my possessions and pride.

With unwavering determination, I selected a facility in Worcester, Massachusetts, as my next destination. My sister, Lisa, came to pick me up to whisk me away to this unfamiliar place.

As I stepped through its doors, an overwhelming sense of trepidation washed over me. This place was a detox center, teeming with 40 to 50 souls, men and women alike, each carrying their unique burdens and battling their own demons. It was an environment where stories of redemption and recovery were etched into the very walls, a sanctuary for those seeking solace on the strenuous path of healing.

I had abstained from alcohol for a couple of weeks by that point and was determined to find peace in life, learn how to survive in life, and go through the challenges life throws at you without depending on alcohol. Though fear clung to me like a shadow, I clung even tighter to any thread of positivity I could find. It was during this period that I found myself at a place called Washburn House in Worcester, a place that offered more than just a fresh start; it offered a lifeline.

Washburn House housed an extended care facility, a sanctuary where I arrived a couple of days after my initial struggle with recovery. Here, I had the potential to stay for up to 90 days, a window of time that would ultimately breathe life back into my weary soul. It was as though an unseen force, a guiding hand, gently steered me forward during those crucial 90 days.

It wasn't a matter of anyone instructing me to make certain choices. No one explicitly told me to venture into the small gym tucked away within those walls, where an elliptical machine waited patiently. It was as if my spirit had grown weary of the old ways, yearning for something new and vibrant. I felt like I had exhausted all other avenues except one: the path to recovery. Desperation had settled deep within me, a longing to rediscover the sensation of feeling fulfilled and satisfied with life.

During this time, I turned to prayer, a practice instilled in me since childhood. My faith, shaped by moments of inexplicable wonder, such as the miraculous births of my daughters, was rekindled. These moments left an indelible mark on my soul, a testament to the profound mysteries of life and the divine presence that guides us through its twists and turns.

Approximately two months into my arduous journey toward recovery, a pivotal moment unfolded. It occurred on an ordinary day, accompanied by the distant echo of music playing in the background. The melodious notes called out to my soul, prompting me to muster the courage to request the person beside me, "May I use your headphones?"

With careful precision, I donned those headphones, and the enchanting melodies of Elton John enveloped me. Instantaneously, a surge of emotions surged through me, sending shivers down my spine and causing goosebumps to arise like newfound life. It was as if I could feel the very essence of the music, bringing a moment of clarity to my hazed life. I felt like the fog had suddenly lifted from my eyes, and I now had a completely different outlook on life.

Initially, I regarded this as a mere phrase, a poetic expression. I watched in genuine awe as the metaphorical fog that had obscured my existence for so long dissipated quite literally. I'm not exaggerating; it felt as though a veil had been lifted from my eyes, revealing a world I had nearly forgotten.

Tears welled up in my eyes, tears of joy and liberation. It was a moment of profound awakening, "Oh, my God," I whispered to myself, overwhelmed by the sheer wonder of it all.

Music had emerged as the catalyst for my rebirth, my resurgence into the realm of the living. I had been ensnared in a perpetual haze, unable to grasp the clarity of life until that day. The transformation was nothing short of miraculous, a transcendent moment that defied explanation.

Fueled by this newfound liveliness, I redirected my focus toward getting in shape. The pounds began to melt away, and I shed approximately 12 pounds during my stay. I found solace in this environment, a sense of belonging that had long eluded me.

However, as the days passed, I was reminded that it was time to transition to the next phase of my recovery journey. A mix of apprehension and determination welled up inside me as I realized that a new chapter was about to begin. "Oh, God, here we go," I thought, preparing myself for the unfamiliar challenges that lay ahead.

The next step was a level of care one notch lower. I had completed the initial level on the site board to detox, and now I found myself at this new stage known as Jeremiah's Inn. It was similar to a sanctuary for my turbulent life. My heart raced with a blend of trepidation and anticipation, for this place was more than just a facility; it was a dual diagnosis haven.

Jeremiah's Inn was an old house with a history that stretched back 150 years, nestled right in the heart of Worcester. It was a place where 30 souls like mine resided, along with a dedicated staff. Walking through its creaking halls, I could sense a palpable sense of community. The kitchen was a hub of activity, where residents gathered to prepare meals and share stories. It wasn't just a house; it was a miniature community of support and camaraderie.

Within these walls, they referred to it as the "social model." Here, the residents of the house played a significant role in governing our shared space. While the clinical team set the rules, we also had a voice, which was a much-welcomed change of pace. We voted on who would do the chores and even took turns cooking dinner. It was a small-scale version of democracy within these four walls.

Now, about the roommates – I had never been a fan of sharing my living space. Growing up as the only boy, I'd always had my room since childhood. So, yes, I despised the idea of having roommates. But life had pushed me into a corner, leaving me with little choice. The alternative was the harsh reality of homelessness. I clung to the tiny glimmer of security that Jeremiah's Inn offered, a place where I could heal and hope to feel whole again.

As I settled in, I opened up about my newfound interest in exercise. I had started on this path during my previous stay, and it had made a remarkable difference. However, with COVID-19 looming, joining a gym was not an option. They were worried, concerned that the outside world might throw me off balance. Yet, all I wanted was a simple thing – to walk. I pleaded with the management, assuring them that I had no intentions of straying from my path of recovery.

During my nine-month stay at Jeremiah's Inn, I walked a staggering 2,300 miles. It was my solace, my therapy, and a testament to the strength I was discovering within myself. Along the way, I shed 115 pounds, a physical transformation that mirrored the profound changes happening within.

There was this one time when the house was put on lockdown due to relentless Covid. We were placed in separate groups and instructed to stay in our rooms with only small intervals of time to eat in the kitchen and go outside and walk, but only on the grounds of the small property.

I became worried about feeling isolated, which was a really bad thing for me during my decline. I needed to walk and was determined. So, I used the half-hour breaks to walk around the house as many times as I could. During that week, I managed to circle the house 750 times, which equated to about 45 miles. I logged all of my calories/ walking/ and eventually cycling distances with apps on my phone and, in this case, my laps around the house. It made the isolation bearable as I got my cherished exercise.

As spring arrived, my sister, Jen, surprised me with a repaired bicycle, a gift that breathed new life into me. But there was a hitch – my driver's license had been revoked, and the journey to reclaim it was still ongoing. Yet, I remained undeterred, determined to keep moving forward on this path to recovery, one step at a time.

Transitioning from primarily walking to embracing biking marked the start of my journey. Approximately a month into my newfound cycling adventure, I took a significant step by moving into a sober house in Massachusetts, a crucial milestone in my path to recovery. The state provided an array of top-notch services, particularly good healthcare, without any financial burden.

Even when dealing with my blood clot issue, they covered all the expenses and delivered exceptional care. This included support for my stay in the recovery house and more. These were welcomed surprises as I had previously received no aid in any form and had to rely solely on myself while struggling with a deadly addiction. I also seized opportunities to enroll in various courses that paved the way for a brighter future. One of these courses led to my certification as a counselor, transforming me from someone seeking help into someone capable of offering it.

Another remarkable opportunity was a QuickBooks accounting class, which I successfully completed, earning a QuickBooks certification at no cost. Additionally, I received a donated car through these services, offering newfound freedom and mobility that felt like a lifeline, supporting my progress.

That's the shortened version of my journey. Now, let's delve deeper into the transformation that unfolded. The countless miles I clocked on my bike amounted to nearly 4,500 miles. I embarked on captivating bike trips, pedaling from Worcester to Cape Cod, sometimes spanning hundreds of miles, where I camped out amid nature's glory. These solo rides unveiled unseen sides of familiar places despite being brought up in the area. I also joined a cycling fundraiser for kids' cancer research. "The Great Cycle Challenge" and raised $2000 for the kids. My photo was shown on the great billboard in Times Square, New York.

On the billboard at Times Square, 2021

The indescribable joy and liberation I experienced during this adventurous time were profound. Recovery isn't a quick fix; it's a complex process. I had spent four decades in the grip of alcohol, which had long-term effects, particularly on my brain. Fortunately, I managed to heal, a testament to the remarkable resilience of the human spirit.

As I gradually emerged from my shell, each step forward unlocked new opportunities. Unexpectedly, one of these opportunities was a job offer in window tinting, a field I had thought I'd never venture into again after letting go of my window tinting business and real estate ventures. It was a chance to start afresh, rebuilding my life one step at a time.

At the age of 57, I found myself considering a new career path as an addiction counselor, an unconventional choice for someone in my stage of life. I was also hired as an RSS (Recovery Support Specialist) at Jeremiah's Inn, where I was in treatment for six months on the weekend night shift. Sadly, one night, someone died during my shift. I found him on his bedroom floor. It made me second-guess what I was doing at first. Unexpectedly, an old competitor contacted me, offering an opportunity in the window tinting industry. Uncertain about diving back in, I ultimately decided to take the leap. Surprisingly, it proved to be a successful venture for about a year and a half.

My work took me from New York City to Florida and across New England. Then, winter arrived, and I received an offer to tint windows in Australia. Wanting to avoid disappointing my colleagues back home, I discussed it with them, knowing that winter was not the ideal time for their business. They were skeptical, but I took a leap of faith.

On January 1st, I landed in Melbourne, Australia, ready to tint windows in the city and its surroundings. My visa lasted for three months. Unfortunately, the job did not unfold as expected. Promises made by the person who hired me could not be kept, and my work did not meet their high standards.

Me during my trip to Australia, Newfoundland

Despite 35 years of experience, I found myself working alongside two exceptional 22 and 23-year-olds who excelled at window tinting. My role diminished, and I became more of an assistant than a tinting specialist.

I persisted for a few weeks and realized that I was owed $3,000, which had not been paid in full. Listening to my instincts, I chose not to quit immediately, as the comfortable apartment and company vehicle provided by my employer seemed worth it.

As the unpaid amount grew, I set a limit. When it remained unpaid, I made the difficult decision to resign. I returned the company van, left a note, and relinquished all belongings, including a full tank of gas. Renting a car, I embarked on an unforgettable two-month journey through Australia and Tasmania.

Living out of my car and occasionally using a low-priced tent and camping gear I purchased, I covered approximately 15,000 kilometers. Words can't fully capture the magnificence of my experiences. It felt like a spiritual awakening, immersing myself in the natural beauty that surrounded me. Australia is truly an incredible country.

During this time, I traveled alone, and it was a remarkable and transformative journey. Beginning in Melbourne, I flew in gliders, explored Queensland, Brisbane, and Sydney, and eventually returned to Melbourne and took a ferry to Tasmania. Each day brought a new adventure, and I was completely captivated by the wonders of this land.

With much cooler weather, I decided against camping in a tent for my Tasmania journey. Initially, I was going to utilize public transportation there. The car rental company didn't allow it on the ferry.

Instead, I opted to rent a second car, an unexpected cost that I covered with some of my savings. I wanted to spend my remaining ten days exploring as much of Tasmania as I could. I spent those nights at various Airbnbs throughout the State.

I spent most days on free beachside campsites with kangaroos and friendly wombats roaming about. It felt almost surreal, like an adventure beyond the wildest imagination. The experience was truly remarkable.

Upon my return home in April, my job with the people who had hired me during my absence abruptly ended. Unfortunately, they struggled to convey their concerns, leaving me disheartened effectively. The contrast with my extraordinary journey was stark.

With no work prospects on the horizon, I decided to fulfill a long-held dream of driving to Newfoundland, the birthplace of my grandmother. I embarked on a solo two-week trip, with most of my nights spent in my trusty tent.

I beheld breathtaking icebergs and briefly connected with my family's roots, enjoying a rejuvenating mini-vacation that made it feel like I was exploring the world year-round.

My journey of exploration started two years ago when I left Jeremiah's. Along the way, I resided in sober houses, which serve as stepping stones for individuals transitioning back into regular life after battling addiction. While they provided financial support, covering my expenses for six months, I soon discovered that each phase of this journey had its unique challenges. I had naively assumed that sober houses implied everyone was genuinely sober, yet I encountered a fellow resident using heroin in the bathroom, and even the house manager seemed to grapple with sobriety.

This marked a turning point for me, as I realized I had no desire to return to drinking, which had once wreaked havoc on my life. I yearned to break free from this environment and move forward. A year and a half ago, I once again moved in with Ron, marking the fourth time we've shared a home.

Ron was actually the very first person I shared a home with when I first moved out of my parent's house, a move that happened way back when I was a wide-eyed 20-year-old. As time passed, Ron and I found ourselves drawn into the thrilling world of skydiving and scuba diving. He was there with me on my first jump into the wild blue skies, a moment that marked the beginning of our adventures. We continued to be roommates for another year, but fate had other plans.

Life has a funny way of circling back. Here we were, four decades later, living together once more in Somerville, Massachusetts, and now in Exeter, New

Hampshire. It almost felt like a reunion with destiny. Living with Ron has been a serendipitous blessing. Our history dates back to when I was just 20, and with a six-year age gap, our bond has only grown stronger over the years.

Currently, I find myself in a role that's a world away from the adventures of my youth. I'm employed as a *Behavioral Health Technician*, or B.H.T, a job I hadn't experienced until August of this year. I'm also still installing window film, but at a minimal level now.

I'm on the flip side now, providing support and assistance to individuals wrestling with addiction. I'm not yet a counselor, but that's my goal. I'm actively working towards it, amassing the necessary clinical experience. It's a new perspective for me, but I'm determined to make a positive impact in this realm.

Reflecting on the journey, it's been a whirlwind of transformations. I've breezed through it quickly, but each stage, each experience, is a brushstroke on the canvas of my life. I'm learning how to articulate these transformations, and it's like weaving a little magic into my story.

My Australian adventure, following my decision to leave my job, was nothing short of extraordinary. It was a journey through erosion, where the ugliness of life revealed its unexpected beauty. I was entranced and captivated by the world around me. Imagine having miles of pristine beaches all to yourself, the waves whispering their secrets just for you.

I walked along cliffs with a sheer drop of a thousand feet to the ocean below. It was a place where solitude could swallow you whole, where the thought of vanishing into the abyss was all too real. A few years earlier, I might have entertained that idea, but not now. The sheer magnificence of it all rekindled a belief in a higher power, in a guiding force. I didn't hear voices, but something changed within me. It was as though the universe itself had aligned to support my journey toward sobriety. It was a profound manifestation, a testament to the power of change when you're truly ready for it.

I was cast adrift, no doubt about it. My journey to recovery was guided by the right kind of help, a specialized approach known as dual diagnosis or co-occurring treatment. This approach targets the intricate relationship between addiction and mental health issues, a link that often goes unnoticed.

You see, addiction and mental health struggles often intertwine like a tangled web. For instance, those grappling with depression might turn to substances like alcohol to numb their pain, seeking a fleeting sense of relief. It's a cycle where one problem fuels the other, creating a vicious loop.

In the past, traditional addiction treatment often resembled a revolving door. They'd detox you and send you home with a stern warning to stay clean, but you'd find yourself right back in the same predicament sooner or later. Why? Because addiction is not just a physical dependency; it's a battle of the mind.

One of my counselors aptly described addiction as a disease that preys on both the mind and free will. You have the freedom to choose, to indulge in those familiar vices, but breaking free from their grasp demands Herculean willpower. It's like trying to shatter a relentless habit that clings to you, gnawing at your resolve.

Breaking free from this cycle is a monumental challenge. It's like scaling a seemingly insurmountable mountain, one that you can't conquer without the right tools and guidance.

So, preparing for the next chapter in this journey means combining the lessons of the past with the hope of tomorrow. It's a legacy of resilience and the promise of brighter days ahead, all nurtured through the power of the right treatment and faith that it will work.

Chapter 12: Leaving a Legacy

It took me many years, to the point of losing everything, to find and start the right treatment. In retrospect, my friends believe that my stubbornness was the reason my treatment was delayed.

While writing this book, my intention is to forge an impactful legacy that guides others through the complexities of overcoming addiction. My personal evolution carried me from the shadowy valleys of substance dependence to a figure of inspiration for those battling similar adversities. I began my path to sobriety with hesitant, modest steps, which gradually transformed into assured, purposeful strides leading me to a life filled with happiness.

A defining yet unexpected milestone on this transformative journey was the honor of having my picture featured on a billboard in Times Square during an event celebrating a cycling fundraiser for kids' cancer research, where I raised $2000.

This acknowledgment was a catalyst for further achievements, such as earning a certification in QuickBooks and revitalizing my window film business, thus widening its scope both domestically and internationally. Moreover, I embarked on a newfound vocational venture as a counselor specializing in addiction.

In the past twelve months, I've traveled four trips to Florida. I've spent three months exploring Australia, plus a 2-week road trip to Newfoundland. I also became a glider pilot, going on 115 flights (international), fulfilling a lifelong dream.

Me during my recent days as a glider pilot

On the other hand, my wife Judy persevered through tough times to continue her education and earn a master's degree in accounting. What I want people to know is that my story is a testament to the resilience and support that can be found in family and the possibilities that can unfold when you work through hardships together. It is a reminder that while addiction can cause a lot of pain and damage, recovery and reconciliation can lead to new beginnings and opportunities to rebuild stronger than before. Keep cherishing and nurturing the positive aspects of life as you continue this journey.

As days passed, my girls got older and began their college life. I felt miserable because I couldn't manage to pay their college fees. On the other hand, my addiction took the best of me. Due to this, one of my girls, Madison, had no choice but to take high-interest loans to pay her fees. She earned her degree in Digital Arts/Photography. Incredibly, my other daughter, Jacie, managed to earn herself a full scholarship and is now a *semper fi* (Always Faithful) Marine. I failed in my marriage and lost my family's emotional support. I also lost some friends and family.

I really hope my story proves to be a light at the end of the tunnel for people who are going through or have gone through such a phase.

In comparison, when I think of the horrible things that people go through all over the world, such as the wars and the torture at the hands of the evil armies of the world, I feel like my experience is nothing compared to people in that situation.

I remember when everything was going downhill, despite heavy drinking, I realized gradually that what I was suffering from was a drinking problem. By no means am I justifying my bad habits, but I just want people to know that no one should take addiction lightly. The longer you wait to treat it, the worse it will get and the harder it will be to recover from it or kill.

Addiction just sucked the life out of me. I felt so hollow on the inside. I felt empty. It felt like everything was destroyed, and in retrospect, everything really was destroyed. The consequences of addiction are worse than what you can probably think of it.

I am on the path to recovery. However, every now and then, I have horrible memories of when people were mad at me. And people were mad at me! I was mad at me!

I was mad at myself to the point of wanting to die, and I thought about it constantly. I would experience terrible guilt and confusion, and there were times when I had blacked out.

I remember driving senselessly one night. I was driving late at night, and I could hear a lot of background noise. My gas gauge showed that my tank was empty, and I had no idea where I was. I just kept driving, and suddenly, I realized that I was in Boston.

Then, another night, I ended up in Framingham, Massachusetts, and it was the same situation where I was low on gas, and I literally had no money. I must say I was lucky enough to scrape up quarters to get myself back to where I was living. I cannot call it home because, indeed, I was homeless. In retrospect, all that senseless driving was just another way of digging my bottomless hole deeper.

I was fortunate enough that it was temporary brain damage. But I was really lost. I felt so helpless and so alone.

I have no idea how this book will sell, yet I am hoping that it will. I'd like every copy to be of use so that a portion of the money that is collected can be sent to a charity that helped me find my way. Perhaps helping homeless people by selling this book can help some.

Addiction is an often misinterpreted affliction that not only affects the individual but also has a profound impact on their loved ones. Unlike a tangible ailment such as cancer, which can be directly targeted with treatments like chemotherapy or surgery, addiction is more intangible and challenging to comprehend.

It can cause a person to act in ways that are perceived negatively by others, who may simply see them as hostile or unpleasant, without understanding the underlying struggle. Furthermore, addiction is fraught with a deep sense of guilt and shame for the sufferer, fueling a relentless and damaging cycle. This psychological burden can make addiction appear more daunting than other medical conditions.

I was neglected in my battle, a common plight for addicts. Groups like Al-Anon offer guidance to those living with addicts, sometimes suggesting they distance themselves. This strategy resulted in my being ignored, fueling my rage and leading to regrettable late-night texts to my family—texts that, once sent, I couldn't retract. This only deepened my need for help, a need I recognized but didn't know how to fulfill. Even my initial therapists were perplexed until the right treatment was found. I had to accept my circumstances, hope for improvement, and utilize the support offered.

Feeling utterly alone, I was so consumed by self-loathing that I often went months without basic self-care. Yet, I continued to exist in a state of mental anguish, weighed down by concern for my family's security and the possibility of their homelessness due to our limited finances. Judy, doing her utmost, was the sole provider of a small income. Her sister, in an act of solidarity, left Georgia to provide support, effectively becoming a housemate for over half a decade to help with household expenses, a necessity since Judy alone couldn't bear the financial burden.

On record, the house was mine, but it didn't feel like it. It had become something else entirely in the wake of these events.

A point came where all I really wanted was peace of mind. I'm not going to lie. There was a point when it almost seemed close to impossible to achieve something as basic as this, but regaining that somehow allowed me to believe in life again.

I'm intrigued by minimalism, like what's portrayed in media and online platforms, though I haven't fully embraced it myself. I tend to allocate my scarce resources towards experiences that offer personal satisfaction and tranquility rather than accumulating things. This pursuit of joy often happens in solitude since I lack a partner to share these moments. Financial challenges have been a constant in my life, marked by high-stakes decisions that sometimes brought success but also led to greater anxiety and depression.

Recently, I channeled my funds into glider flying, an activity that has had a profound positive impact on my mental health. It requires intense concentration and engages my mind in ways I hadn't felt capable of since my struggles four years prior. Gliding, with its intricate maneuvers and the serene backdrop of nature, has reignited a lifelong passion for aviation that began with my first flight at 14.

Now, I reside in a mobile home with affordable rent at a fraction of the average in the area, thanks to my generous and caring friend, Ron, who was also my first roommate nearly 40 years ago. I have no intention of moving any time soon.

At 59, I'm starting anew, cognizant of the need to continue working possibly into my 70s. I'm planning and contemplating a transition from manual work to a career in counseling—a field I could continue in well into old age. My goal is to secure a comfortable life, focused not on luxury but on engaging in activities I cherish and perhaps exploring new hobbies.

I hope this book provides hope to those who are struggling and teaches enough about what should be known about addiction, including the dark and the bright side.

2023, My year of amazing global, alcohol-free adventures!

Printed in Great Britain
by Amazon

43952294R00089